Playing the Recorder

CLIFF TOBEY

Amsco Music Publishing Company, New York
Music Sales Limited, London, W.1

Book design by Jean Hammons and Tara Collins

© 1970 Amsco Music Publishing Company
33 West 60th Street, New York, N.Y. 10023

Music Sales Limited
78 Newman Street, London, W.I.

International Standard Book Number: 0-8256-2146-1
Library of Congress Card Catalogue Number: 73-84933

Contents

Foreword, 5

Session I, 6
   The Instrument
   Initial Fingering
   Breathing
   Producing the Tone
   Tonguing
   Time Keeping

Interlude I, 11
   More Finger Positions
   Relaxation
   First Songs

Session II, 14
   New Notes
   Low C
   Practicing Scales
   New Songs
   Playing by Ear

Interlude II, 17
   More Songs
   Breathing
   Rhythm

Session III, 19
   Reading Notes
   The Staff
   Time Signature
   Reading Songs

Interlude III, 24
   Finger Exercises
   Signs and Symbols
   Song Practice

Session IV, 27
   The Eighth Note
   Counting Time
   Dotted Notes

Interlude IV, 35
   Rests
   New Notes

Session V, 38
   Scales

Interlude V, 42
   The Fermata
   Triplets

Session VI, 44
   New Sharped Notes
   Flatted Notes

Interlude VI, 47
   Accidentals
   Naturals

Session VII, 49
   Tempo

Interlude VII, 51
   International Songs

Session VIII, 53
   Polishing
   Legato Tonguing

Interlude VIII, 56
   New Note Values

Session IX, 58
   Transposing

Interlude IX, 60
   Signs and Symbols

Session X, 61
   Rounds

Interlude X, 63
   Composing Melodies

Appendix A, 65
   Fingering Chart

Appendix B, 66
   Musical Terms

Appendix C, 68
   The Key Signature

Appendix D, 70
   Care of The Recorder
   Tuning The Recorder

Bibliography, 71

Foreword

At least one problem is solved for the person who takes up the recorder: the problem of noisy practice sessions. In the interest of the sprouting musician friends and relatives year after year patiently bear the sound of banging drums and blasting tubas assuring one and all through clenched teeth that "Of course it doesn't bother me." With the delightfully quiet tone of the recorder no such problem exists. One can practice endlessly and keep his neighbors friendly.

When starting this book I had in mind writing it for the benefit of those with no musical training who felt they would like to have some form of musical expression. Being especially aware of the problems faced by the beginner I have attempted to unsnarl the meandering threads of music notation in such a way that the learner would not suddenly find himself confronted by great gaps of information over which he could not leap. All the details of note reading, scales, counting of beats and other technical facts have been carefully woven into the lessons in a manner, it is hoped, whereby the player will pass from one level to the next with a minimum of problems.

Because of its basically simple design the recorder without a doubt is one of the easiest instruments in the world to play. Yet it is a professional instrument with a range of over two octaves and is a natural for the beginner, being as it is a good initial instrument with which to enter the world of music and having as it does a refreshing personality in its own right.

There are two types of recorder in circulation today. One is generally termed the "English" and the other the "German." The first is probably the more popular and can be recognized by the two sets of small double holes at the lower end of the instrument. Both types have the same fingerings except for some small differences which are pointed out in the book.

I would recommend that the beginner purchase a recorder with English (or "Baroque") fingering.

Finally, if it were possible to sit down with each new player and offer a bit of advice about using this book I would say, above all take your time. It's safe to say we don't learn such a thing as music by leaping impatiently ahead, slapping one detail on top of another like a mason frantically trying to build a wall before the sun goes down. Rather we bloom slowly in an integrated way, nursed along by the obscure logic of nature, more like a ripening watermelon.

I could not possibly thank enough the people who gave their time, knowledge and friendly counsel in the preparation of this book for publication. I can only hope they realize how helpful they have been. I'm especially grateful to Donald L. Brooks, Keith McClelland, Frank Vento, Lawrence R. and Judithann Johnson, Frank MacIntosh and Gene Weintraub.

Cliff Tobey

Session I

Recorders are generally made of wood, but if you don't have an instrument at this time it would be better to get an inexpensive plastic model. Wooden ones are available in the low price range but they're not to be trusted. The paint which usually covers them wears off (in your mouth), the separate parts don't fit well together and the tone is a bit lifeless. There are several plastic instruments selling from $1.50 to $3.50, among them the Dolmetsch soprano recorder, pictured here. It's made of a durable synthetic material.

These plastic instruments will do very well at the beginning. Later, when you start to play for others you'll want a better model.

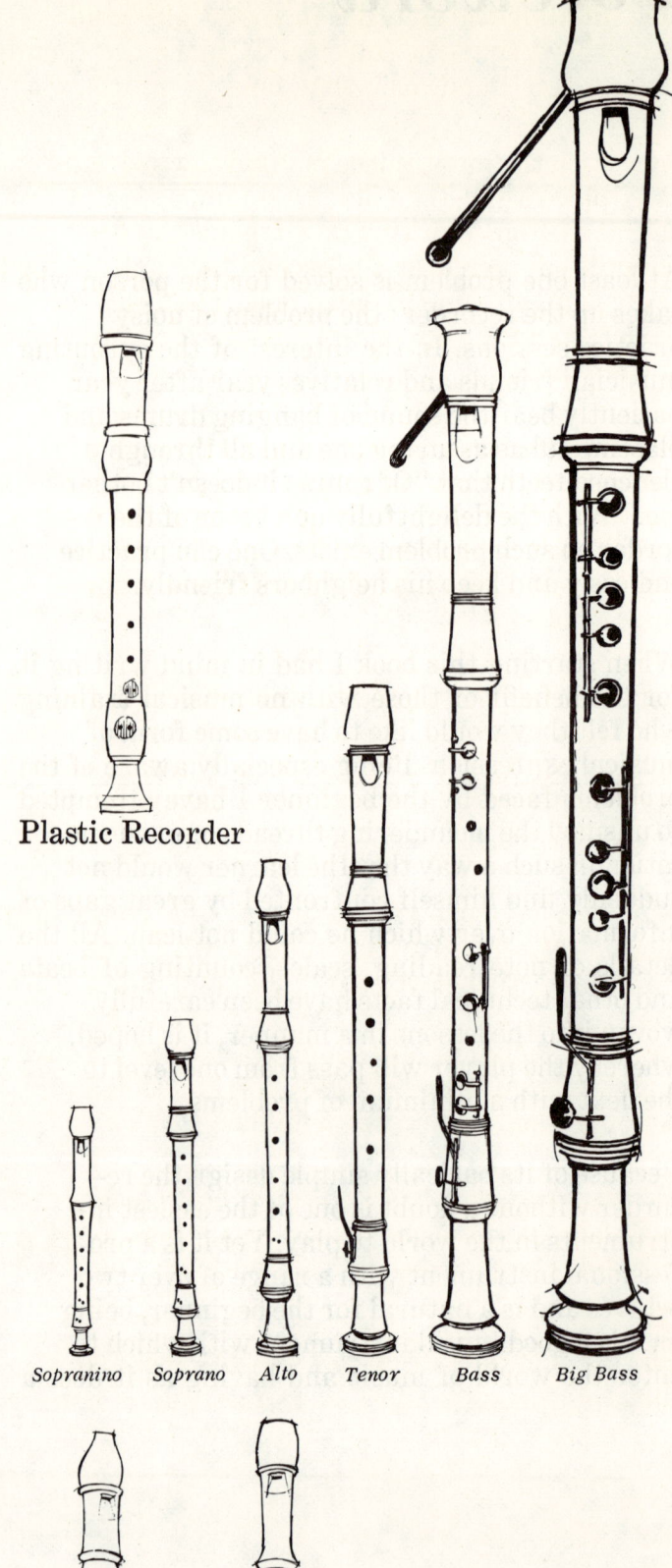

Plastic Recorder

There are several sizes of recorders ranging from the "sopranino" to the "big bass." The smallest produces tones of the highest pitch. We're going to be concerned with only one, the size next to the smallest: the soprano. This is the popular model. It's the easiest to finger, fits the hand nicely and has a pleasant tone.

Sopranino   Soprano   Alto   Tenor   Bass   Big Bass

The two recorders pictured here look different but they're essentially the same. The one in Fig. A has three parts. The lower part (called the "foot") may be turned slightly left or right to fit the length of the individual pinky when the fingers are covering the holes. The Fig. B recorder, in two parts, is made to a standard size and is not adjustable.

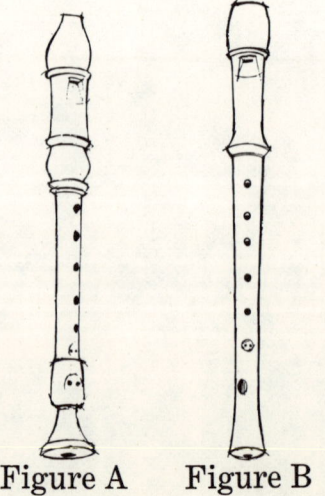

Figure A   Figure B

Before attempting to produce a tone, let's get the feel of the instrument. On the back there's one hole. Holding the recorder in your right hand (anywhere near the lower end) place the thumb of your left hand over that hole.

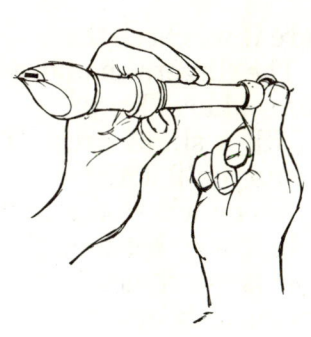

Now with the mouthpiece pointed toward your face, place your 1st (index) finger over the first hole at the top. Working down, place the 2nd (middle) finger over the second hole and the 3rd (ring) finger over the third hole. That's all for the left hand. (Your pinky does nothing but wave at the world.)

If we wanted an easy way of picturing what you've done we could draw a series of circles to represent the holes, the black being those covered and the white those not covered. (The single black circle at the top left of the figure is the thumb hole.)

Let's put the right hand to work. Keeping the left hand holes covered, check to see what's left. Four holes, right? If you're thinking these holes will be covered by the fingers of your right hand, you're correct.

Now you have one thumb left. It will go the only place it conveniently can, underneath the recorder directly below your right hand index finger. This will support the instrument. Everything should be quite comfortable now. You might lift your fingers one or two at a time, popping them up and down on the holes.

(If your recorder has two small holes inside each large one at the lower end, forget them for the moment. Cover them entirely with the two lower fingers.)

Our black and white circles will now look like this:

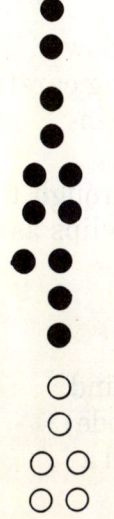

We're about ready to make a tone. First, remove all fingers except those shown in the diagram. (Keep your right thumb in place.)

It might be helpful right here if we check the how of covering the holes. The fingers should not be straight up and down like soldiers. They should be almost flat but with a slight arch. If you'll look at your fingerprints you'll notice a small "whirlpool" on each finger where the little lines come together. About half way between that point and the tip of the finger is the "touch" point. This "pad" will snuggle nicely over the hole like an egg in an egg-cup. Bounce the fingers around a bit and move them back and forth. You'll feel when they fit correctly. Relax the fingers. Don't squeeze, *but be sure the entire hole is covered.* Leaky edges produce real funny noises from the recorder.

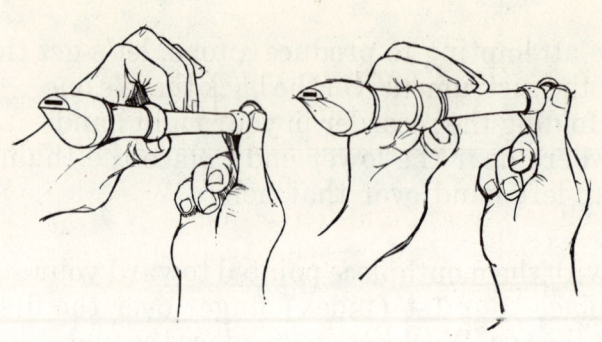

See the man over there on the right about to blow his top? That's the way you don't, don't do it. The recorder is not blown like a trumpet or a balloon. Very little air pressure is needed. To demonstrate for yourself how little, hold the recorder about an inch from your mouth, pucker up as if you were about to whistle and direct a small stream of air into the mouthpiece. Notice how a sound can be produced with even this minimum amount of air pressure.

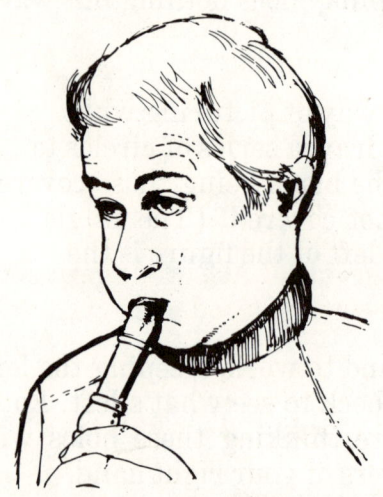

Now to the tone. Glance down to see where the fingers of your right hand are located. Since they will not be covering holes at this point they should be about an inch above each hole. O.K? Place the tip of the mouthpiece about a quarter of an inch into your mouth. Let's stress that point. About a quarter of an inch. No more. The natural tendency is to take a good bite, but this causes the muscles of the lips to bunch and the jaws to become tense, adding to a natural desire to over-blow.

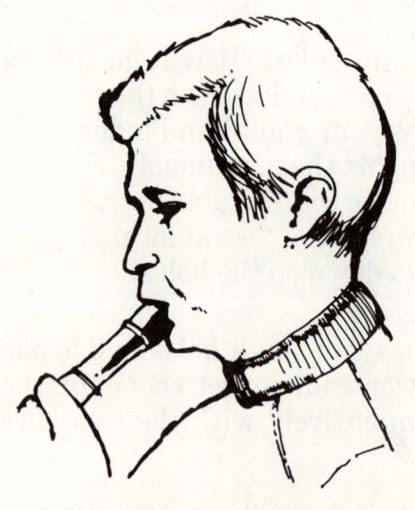

Lay the tip of the mouthpiece on your lower lip, placing your upper lip gently on top being careful that the tongue and teeth don't touch the instrument.
Inhale a medium size breath of air (through the mouth, not the nose) and then form the lips as if you were about to say the word "when."

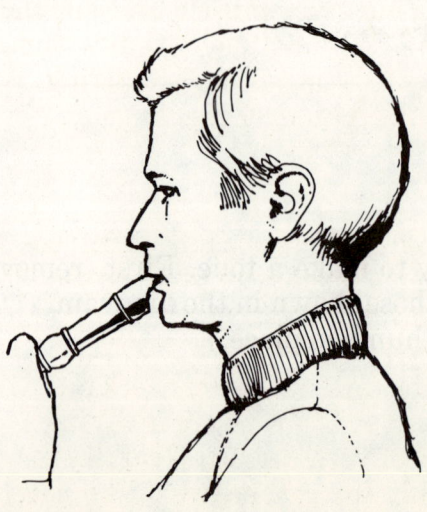

Take time here. Get the image in your mind. Relax the lips and now (before you explode) release the air through the mouthpiece in a steady, flowing stream.

Easy, now. Don't push too much or the tone will be ragged, but be sure the stream of air is strong enough not to be weak and wobbly. You're looking for a nice, gentle stream and not a gush. Practice awhile, making sure your lips are not bunched and that the recorder is only about a quarter of an inch into your mouth.

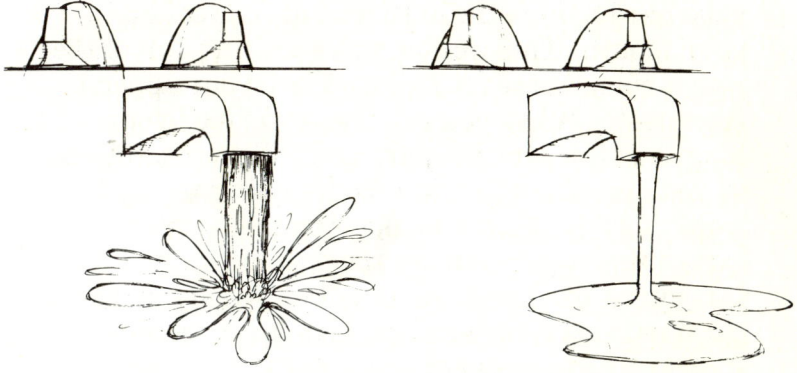

After you've practiced a bit, take the recorder from your mouth and check your fingers. Are the left hand fingers really covering the holes? Move them about until you're certain they're settled over the holes completely with medium pressure. No leaky edges? Are your right hand fingers clear of the bottom four holes, not dragging across the edges? How about the left thumb? Covering the hole on the back? Are all fingers and thumbs nice and relaxed? Good.

Let's do a bit more checking. Sitting, for instance. To get a clear passage for the movement of breath you should be sitting straight, leaning forward a bit with the shoulders up, not slumped. Not too far up; comfortable but not strained. The recorder should be pointed downward, aimed just above the point of your knee, with your chin level.

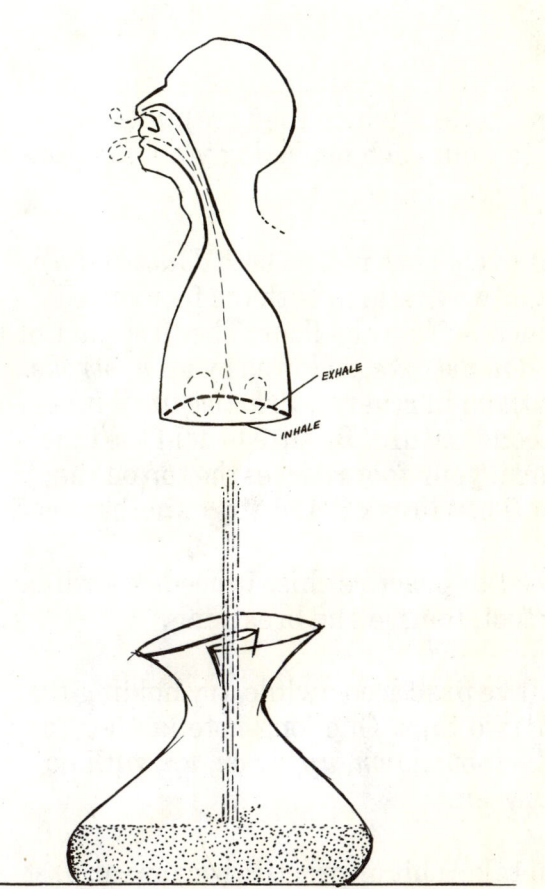

The purpose of these sticky details about position is to arrange all of your "innards" to make it easy for the air to reach the bottom of your lungs so the diaphragm will operate.

This is natural breathing, exactly what you want for playing the recorder. When you run out of air while playing and quickly take another breath (repeat: through the mouth) this gulp of air should rush to the bottom of your lungs, like filling a sandbag. This gives muscle and support to the column of air. Why not try it a few times without the recorder? Breathe deeply, making sure the air goes to the bottom of the lungs.

After you've checked finger position, sitting position and breathing, get ready to produce the tone again. Recorder in place?

Before breathing the tone, mentally check the position of your tongue. Chances are it's lying relaxed on the floor of your mouth. We'd like to move it around a bit (or rather, we'd like *you* to move it around!). Search with it until you find your hard palate, the hard part of the roof of your mouth. The section we're looking for is the rough ridge at the front, just above your upper front teeth. When you say the word "too" your tongue will leave this part and fall to the bottom of your mouth. (Try it.) We're going to use this word "too" in producing notes on the recorder except that we'll shorten the spelling to "tu." So far you've produced the tone in a steady stream, but now release the air, breaking up the steady stream with a series of short "tu's," one for each note.

This is called *tonguing* the instrument and it's done for every note you make on the recorder except for some special ones we'll get to later.

Practice a few of these "tu" tones, four or five on each breath, then nine or ten. Check all points: breathing, relaxation, finger positions.

If you'd like to try producing these tones (let's call them "notes," which they are) with a rhythm, tap out each one using your foot, one tap for each note.

Important: *One tap* means both *down* and *up*. This beat always starts with the foot raised several inches from the floor. The first part of the beat is a *downstroke*, followed by an *upstroke*. Don't do them in reverse. Practice until it becomes second nature. Be sure to hold the tone steady until your foot reaches the top on the upstroke. Then break it and start another beat.

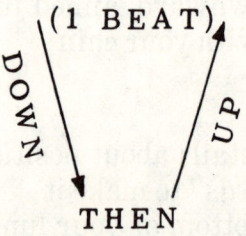

You'll need to practice this. It needs coordination between foot, tongue and breathing.

After you've practiced awhile, try holding the notes for two taps. One long note lasting for two taps of the foot: *down, up, down, up*, with no break between.

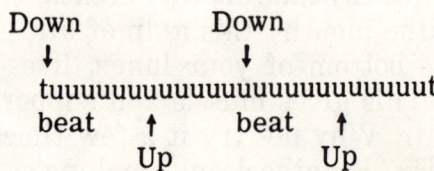

This will take a bit of practice because at first the little "devil" (or whatever it is) inside of you will want to break the note after the first tap, but show him who's boss and keep the air pumping right through the two beats.

Then try holding the notes for three beats. At first you'll want to break after the second beat (because you've been practicing it that way), but *down, devil, down*. Hold it three beats!

Up to holding it four? No? Well, never mind. You deserve a break anyway.

Interlude I

In the last session we urged you to sit straight for good breathing. Why not flop back now, put your feet up and practice a whole series of "tu's?" Of course this is bad for breathing and you mustn't....ahem...do it all the time, but who's looking? If you've got your shoes off, feet on a chair or footstool, you can keep time waving your big toe.

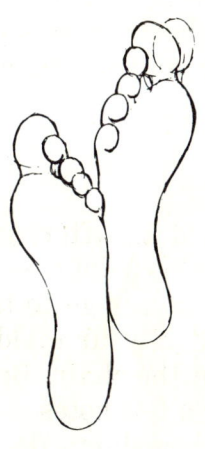

While doing this you can begin to vary the pitch of the notes by lifting the fingers one or two at a time. Let's do it this way: We'll give a symbol to each pitch level so we can identify it.

The note you're making with the top four holes covered (index, middle, ring finger and thumb) we'll call G.

By lifting the bottom finger, only the three top holes are covered and this we'll call A.

When you lift the finger do it quickly and cleanly with a snap, being careful not to start the next tone before you lift the finger or you'll get a click. Coordinate the tone and fingering so you get a nice, clean note.

Then by lifting the middle finger, only the two top holes are covered. This we'll identify as B.

A series of three notes: G A B.

Now play four tu's on G (one tap of the foot for each, down and up). Do it rhythmically.

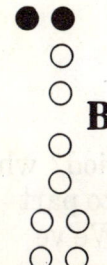

11

Climb up to A by lifting the ring finger (quick and clean!) and play four notes.

  A **A** **A** **A**

Lift the middle finger and play four B's.

  B **B** **B** **B**

Practice this a few times, then try going from the bottom G to the top B. Then B to G, then G to B again, then B to A, A to G. Check to be sure you're popping your fingers up and down, not dragging them.

  G **B** **G** **B** **A** **G, etc.**

Don't forget to grab a small gulp of air after, and sometimes during each series. At this point we should say, "Don't forget to let the air go to the bottom." But this will be difficult if your middle is bent; if you're leaning back in the chair. Best way is to test it for yourself. Play a few notes with your middle "folded," shoulders slumped, then sit up straight and try a few. See how easily the air passes in and out in the straight position?

Here's a good point to take off on your own. Skip all around those three notes from one to the other. Hold some notes for one beat of your toe (down and up), others for two, three, four.

If some of the notes are a bit "off" during this exercise check to see that your fingers are covering the holes completely (the thumb, too, of course). Keep that good, steady stream of air going, not too hard, not too easy. Relax the lips, jaw, throat, fingers.

We'll complete this rest period (rest period? who rested?) by arranging our three notes into part of a familiar melody, "*Yankee Doodle.*" We've altered the last note slightly to end the phrase comfortably. Each note should be one beat except the final A in the first line and the two final G's in the second. Hold these two beats each.

  G **G** **A** **B** **G** **B** **A (2)**
  Yan - kee Doo - dle went to town

  G **G** **A** **B** **G (2)** **G (2)**
  Ri - ding on a po - ny

Like to try one more melody? *Merrily We Roll Along* is good. You could probably pick this one out yourself, but in case you stumble along the way, the notes will be supplied but not the words.

Hold each note one beat except where the (2) or (4) shows it to be that number of beats.

B	A	G	A	B	B	B (2)
A	A	A (2)				
B	B	B (2)				
B	A	G	A	B	B	B (2)
A	A	B	A	G (4)		

Be sure to make a "tu" tone for each note. Do not, as some beginners are apt to do, make a series of "whooo" or "whistle" tones. Bad habits can become set in this way. Remember: A *tu* for each *tone*! Say it nine times an hour, and more if necessary. Ready, everybody? A *tu* . . . .

Play your song slowly at first, then bring it up to the usual speed. Don't forget to check finger coverage, steady stream of air, relaxation. Finally, after practicing, try to play both melodies without looking at the notes. This is "playing by ear," half the fun of playing the recorder.

Session II

First thing, we'll find a couple more notes in addition to G, A, B. We're going up the scale. We'll call the first one (above B) C. The fingering is shown on the right. You'll see what must be done: remove finger No. 1 (index) and No. 3 (ring). That leaves the thumb and No. 2 finger. Try that note a few times.

Finding the next note up – D – is easy. Simply remove your thumb, leaving only the middle finger over hole No. 2. (We hope you've kept your right hand thumb in place or the recorder will do what comes naturally and fall on the floor!)

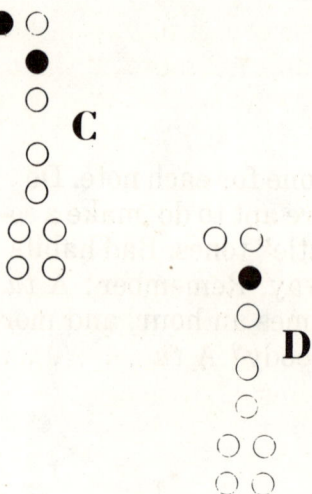

Practice going from one note to another:

C D C D C D C D C D. etc.

Start with G and run up to D, playing all the notes you have. Then come back down. Do it a few times without keeping time, then start beating, holding some notes one beat, two, three, four. Loosen up and have fun doing it.

D C D C D C D C D C. etc.

You'll notice it's beginning to sound like a real scale, which it is. Or at least part of a scale, like the one you learned way back in early grammar school: Do–Re–Mi–Fa–Sol, etc. Remember? You always started on a certain key note which the teacher blew on a pitchpipe. Then you sang the scale or a song.

Let's go back to *Merrily We Roll Along* and change a couple notes now that we have more to play. Looking back you'll see that in the third line we gave you three B's. That's one way to play it. The other is with one B and two D's.

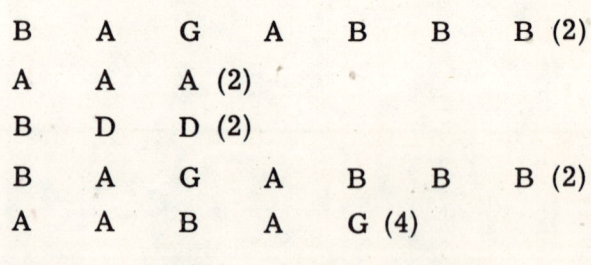

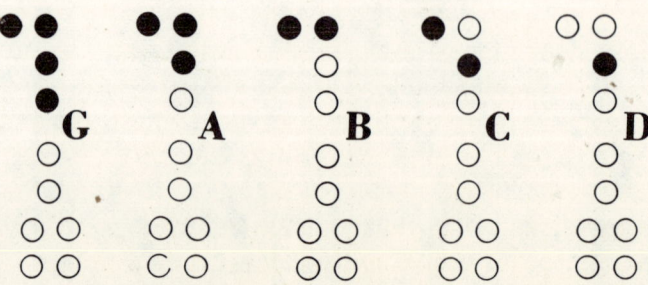

We'll take a look at all the notes you have so far, using the handy circle notation system.

Your left hand has been doing all the work. Time to get after the right. We're going to move along quickly now and pick up the rest of the main notes down the scale.

To reach the next one you have to do a bit of fancy finger work. Looking at the chart you'll see that everything is covered except the third hole from the bottom. That's the next note: F.

You can see what's necessary going from G to F. Cover all the bottom holes except the third at the same moment. Otherwise the note won't be clean. Practice it.

Next on the way down: E.

No trouble with that? O.K. Next: D. Sound familiar? It should. It's the same note as the D above except it's an octave lower (eight notes, counting the first note, D, as one).

Finally, the bottom: C. Let's call it low C since it, too, is an octave lower.

Low C gives most beginners difficulty in getting a clear note. So, a few tips on producing it. First, make sure the holes are completely covered. The lowest one must be watched very carefully. It may be necessary to press quite firmly with your pinky. Also, you can do something you normally do when you reach for a low note in singing (you can't sing? Good grief!). Drop your head an inch or so and open your throat wide. To get the idea of this, sing a very high note, then a low, low one. See how your head naturally dips for that low note. Several things happen and one of them is this: the pressure of the breath gets less because the "tunnel" gets larger. That's what we want for that *low* C note: less force in the stream of air. So relax, breathe easy and practice.

Practice? Right. That's the thing to do now. Run up and down that scale a few million (well, not quite) times. Begin with low C and go up to high D and back. You'll have to tread carefully awhile around that F, but you'll get it in time. Check everything along the way: finger coverage, breathing, relaxation. All musicians, even those with years of experience, practice scales to develop nimble fingers and coordination. Make it part of your routine.

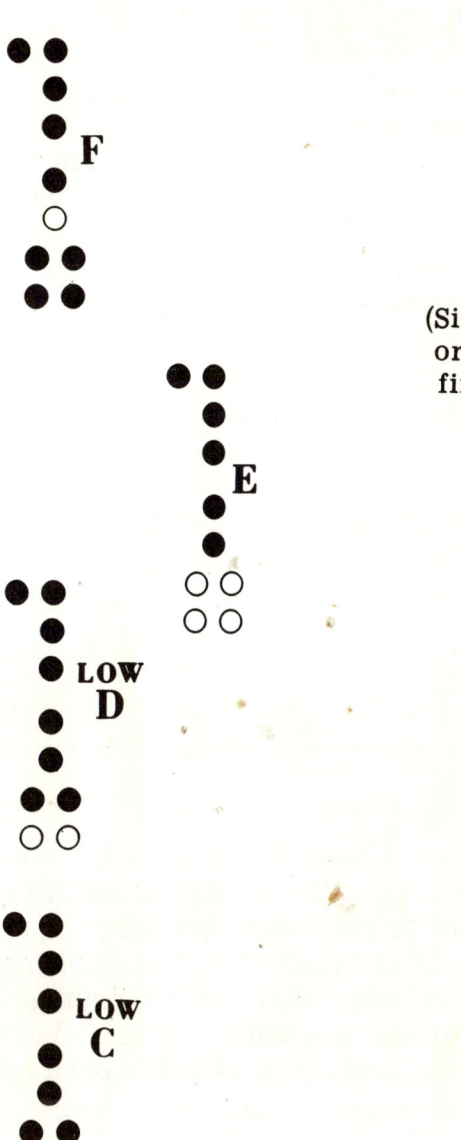

(Single Hole or German fingering)

If you begin on low C and run up to high C, you'll now have a complete scale: Do–Re–Mi–Fa–Sol–La–Ti–Do, eight notes. This will sound complete and "right" and familiar. But if you start on D and go up, step by step, to high D, it will not sound like a scale. It won't sound right, even though there are eight notes. This is one of those little mysteries of music we'll make clear in later lessons. For the moment pay no attention.

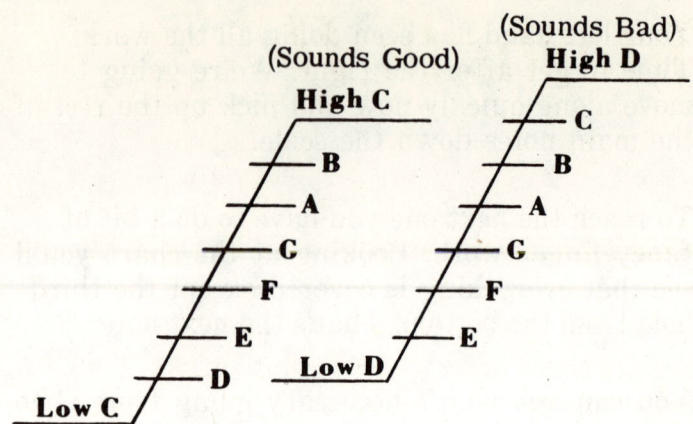

We'll complete this lesson by finding one new note and then try a couple of songs.

As you've probably noticed, low C, (with all the holes covered) is the lowest note on your recorder. But we can go up. So let's build another note: high E.

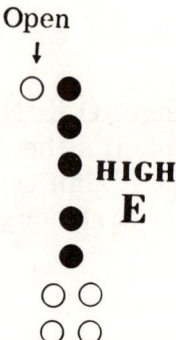

To get this one, arrange your fingers to make low E. Then simply remove the left hand thumb and there you have it.

Remember we mentioned that to get a low note it was necessary to open the throat? Same thing is true in reverse: to get those high notes, squeeze the throat a little and push with that diaphragm. This gives power and muscle to the stream of air by forcing it through a smaller "tunnel." You'll judge for yourself exactly how hard to push and how much to squeeze.

If that low C still sounds a little shaky, remember to (1) open your throat wide, (2) "ease" the air through the recorder and (3) press firmly with your pinky (more than for the other notes). Play by ear any or all of these songs.

1. *Oh, Susanna* (Oh, I come from Alabama). Starting note is low C. Highest note you'll reach is A.

2. *Joy To The World.* Start at high C. Highest note: high C.

3. *Frere Jacques.* Start at G. Highest note: high E.

Interlude II

Here are three more songs to play by ear. They're good practice.

1. *Alouette*. Start at G. Highest: high E.

2. *Long, Long Ago*. Start: G. High: high E.

3. *Twinkle, Twinkle Little Star*. Start at low C. high: A.

It's not necessary on these ear pieces to keep strict time. Beat it out but don't worry if it isn't right; you'll have counting exercises in later lessons. The finger exercise is the thing now, plus ear training in finding those notes.

Have you had some difficulty knowing where to breathe as you've played these songs? Everyone does at the start.

In some (but not all) music written for the recorder, breathing places are marked, usually by a comma, check mark or slash. They occur at natural places such as the end of a musical phrase or sentence.

, or ✓ or /

Speaking of breathing: most beginners have a tendency to use too much air on the recorder. It probably wouldn't hurt to try cutting down your breathing pressure by half. Then, cut it again by half. A very little amount of air is needed. Try playing so softly you'll barely be able to hear the tone. Then build it a little. Develop the ability to play either softly or loudly.

A final thought about keeping the rhythm. Most convenient way is tapping the foot. Another is to have a friend make like a conductor, waving a baton or pencil or a finger. Still another is keeping time to the tick of a clock. The best way is by using a metronome, a small clocklike machine on which the tempo (speed) can be set. It produces loud rhythmic ticks to which the time is kept.

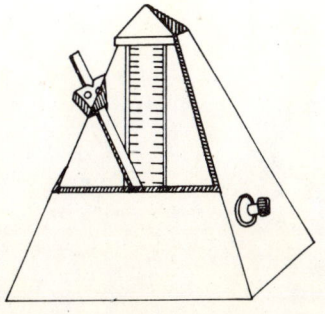

One of the pleasures of the recorder is playing it with someone else who plays.

It's a very old instrument going way back in history. There have been long periods when it was popular and everybody who was anybody played it. There have been periods when the popularity faded. Recently there's been a revival (everything in life, they say, goes in cycles). You and I are part of that revival.

If you have a friend who might like to play, why not invite him or her to practice right along with you? There are many ways to do it. Possibly studying each lesson together, finding the notes, beating out the time. Then, after each person has practiced alone, meeting again, playing the last lesson and starting the new one.

This way you'll be prepared for group playing. There are many groups around the country and getting to be more. Also, there are song books written especially for two soprano recorders.

Playing an instrument is one of the great pleasures of life. It's never too late to start.

Session III

To make one beat you tapped your foot down and then up. And you played a tone on your recorder to fit the length of that beat.

In written music that one beat is represented by a symbol: the quarter note (♩). (In some cases it isn't, but let that wait.)

The quarter note can be made short by tapping your foot quickly or it can be S–T–R–E–T–C–H–E–D by tapping slowly, but it's still a quarter note and gets one beat. Speed, or tempo, does not change the nature of it.

Let's put four of these quarter notes in a row. Now tap them out: Down, Up; Down, Up; Down, Up; Down, Up. There is a break at the "top" of each beat, making four notes.

If we want one note to last the length of those four quarter notes (and we do!) we use the *whole* note, and egg shaped white circle (o). The whole note is *one long note* (with no "breaks") lasting four taps of the foot. 4 quarter notes are four *separate* notes.

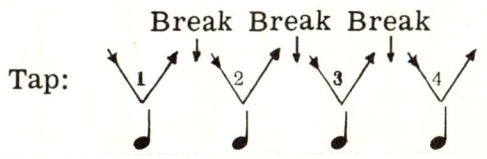

The other symbol widely used in written music is the *half* note, a white circle with a stem (𝅗𝅥). It's counted with *two* beats: twice as long as the quarter note, half as long as the whole note.

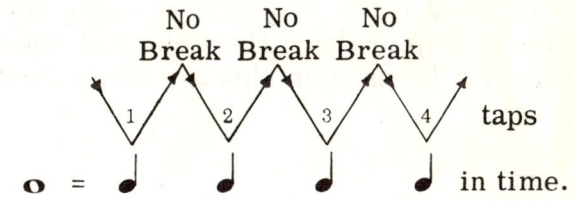

We'll put it to use, using *Yankee Doodle*. Don't use the recorder just yet. Sing the words.

♩ ♩ ♩ ♩ ♩ ♩ 𝅗𝅥
Yan - kee Doo - dle went to town

Use one beat (down and up) for all those quarter notes and two beats for the half note at the end. (Do it fast or slow. It doesn't make any difference.)

Try it a few times to see if you get the swing of it.

19

Think about that half note for a moment. Since two quarter notes equal a half note, why not use them instead? Because the word "town" has one "tone" which must last for two beats. If quarter notes were used, there would be two tones. So the half note says: "The tone that goes with this symbol must last for two beats and these two beats do not go up or down the scale; they stay at the same pitch level."

The whole note stays the same, but the tone lasts for four beats.

Let's suppose you never heard of the song *Yankee Doodle*. If we take the first phrase just as it's written here and try to play it on the recorder (starting on G) what would happen? We'd have to play it all on the same pitch because it doesn't tell us how to go up and down the scale!

♩ ♩ ♩ ♩ ♩ ♩ ♩
Yan - kee Doo - dle went to town

This is where the staff comes in. The staff has five lines and four spaces, so if we write a note on each line or space we can cover nine steps up or down the scale. Not enough. More note levels than this are often used.

So we add bits of lines above or below called *leger lines*.

The lines and spaces on the staff are each given an identity using the first seven letters of the alphabet, a, b, c, d, e, f, g.

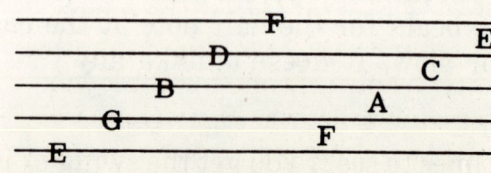

20

If we want to go further up or down we use the leger lines and the same letters of the alphabet over and over.

(Have you begun to suspect these letters have something to do with those you have learned? Right. The first note on your soprano recorder––low C– is located on the first *leger line* below the staff. The high E you learned is on the last space of the staff at the top.)

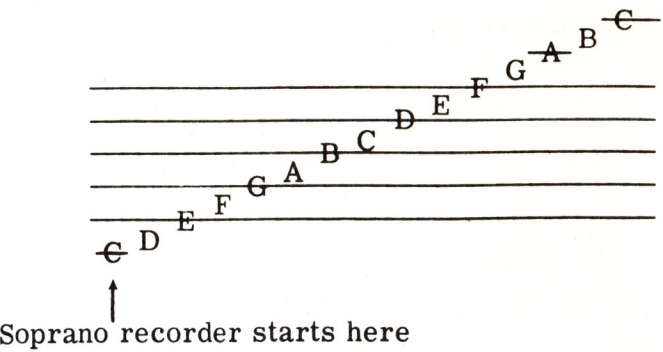
Soprano recorder starts here

It will take some time to get all those letter names straight, but don't let that stop you. We'll only be using four or five for awhile and you can refer back to this page for others. Or, better yet, make yourself a sketch and keep it handy for reference.

Let's take away the letters and put some notes on the staff.

Besides the notes, three things have been added.

1. The breathing mark (,).

2. Some vertical lines called *bars*. The spaces between the bars are called *measures*. (Sometimes, for convenience, the measures are called bars.)

   Bar   Bar
   |← measure →|

3. The *Clef* sign: 𝄞   This gives us quite a bit of information. The tail inside the sign curls around the second line: G.

It also tells us we'll look for the staff which has this sign when we want to play the soprano recorder. The G clef staff is where the notes for this instrument are written (also for the guitar, upper part of the piano, violin, etc.). This staff is for the upper (higher) register. There's another staff below this one for the lower register called the *Bass* (base) clef with its own sign.

Great Staff

21

The G clef says that the second line (with the tail around it) will always be G. By starting there and following the letters of the alphabet up or down you can tell the letter name of the line or space immediately.

One more bit of information about music notation and you'll be able to start playing.

Back to our staff with the notes: look at the measures (8 of them).

They divide the music into convenient sections for easy reading. To make it even easier, the composer tells us two things about them. He does it by putting two numbers on the staff, one above the other, after the Clef sign. In this piece we'll use $\frac{2}{4}$.

The top number tells us how many beats there will be in each measure (2 here). The bottom number indicates which note will get *one beat*; in this case it will be the quarter (/4) note. Later, you'll see how other notes get that basic beat. Here, then, we'll have 2 beats in each measure and every quarter note will get one beat. Together, the two numbers are called the *time signature* or the *metric signature*.

We're ready to play (did you recognize it?) *Yankee Doodle* (with the altered note).

G G A B G B A
G G A B G G

Work carefully. You won't be able to read quickly at first. You'd be a pure genius if you could! Like all who have "gone the route" you'll have to be patient until you get all the essentials straight. You'll be amazed how fast they come.

Remember that in $\frac{2}{4}$ time the accent is on the first beat. You lean on the first beat rather heavily and less on the second (*ONE* two, *ONE* two). Give a full beat to every quarter note and two full beats to every half note.

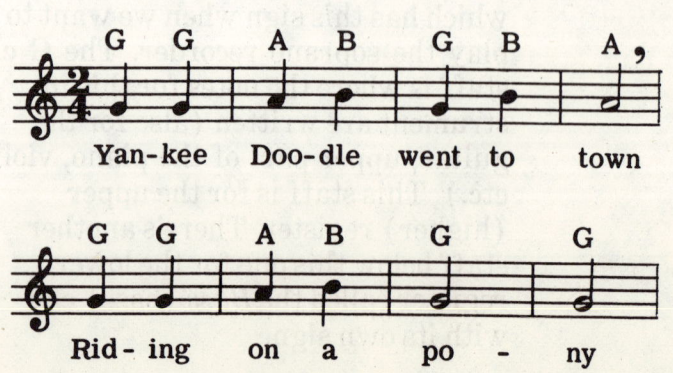

22

Try *Merrily We Roll Along* now. There's nothing new in this except it's in $\frac{4}{4}$ time.

Four beats to the measure and the quarter note gets one beat. So the half note gets what? Right, right.

Accent is on the first beat and a bit less on the third beat. *ONE* two *three* four.

Hold that *Whole* note four full beats.

Have you wondered why some notes are written stems up and others down? Neatness, that's all. Below B they're written up, above B written down. On the B line they can be written either way.

Notice the very end of the staff. There's a *Double Bar* instead of a single. This means it's an important ending, in this case, the end of the song!

Interlude III

Here's a bit of information about the soprano recorder you can file away: it's called a C recorder because it starts on the C note. It's tuned to the key of C. (Later, when you study scales you'll understand that better.) The notes for the soprano recorder are written starting on the first leger line below the staff (middle C on the piano). But even though the notes are written there, the sound for the soprano actually starts an octave above middle C. The reason? What would happen if the written notes started where the sound does? Playing *up* from there many of the notes would be in the clouds, above the staff. Very difficult to read. So the soprano recorder music is written an octave lower than it sounds.

How would you like to do some plain old finger exercises? You know, to practice moving up and down the scale? And keeping time? (You wouldn't? Why not?)

It's a good idea before you start playing to tap yourself a "free" measure just to set the beat.

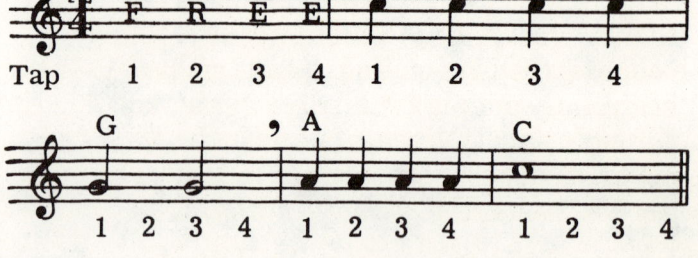

How fast or slow will you play? Start playing slowly and when you know the exercises a little "by ear" pick up the tempo.

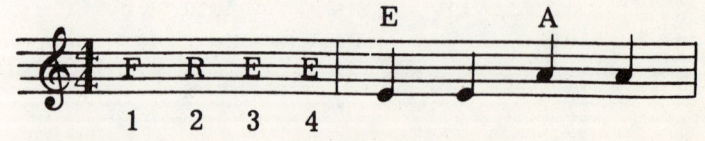

Let's switch to $\frac{2}{4}$ time, two beats to the measure, the quarter note getting one beat.

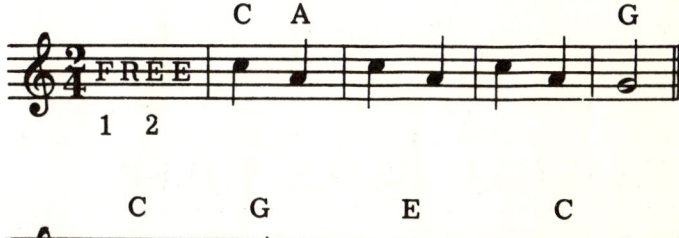

Here's one written a little fancier. It introduces two new features, the *Repeat* and the *First & Second Endings*.

This is what you do: play merrily along as usual. When you reach the *Repeat* sign you have come to the *First Ending*. Those two dots, which conclude the first ending, mean: go back to the beginning and play it all over again, but this time through, skip the measure under the No. 1 canopy and play the measure (or measures) under the No. 2 sign, the *Second Ending*.

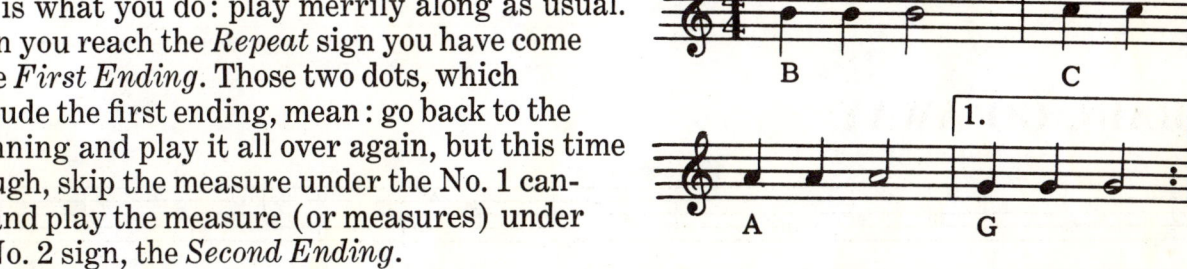

It's possible to have a repeat without a second ending. In this case, go to the beginning, play right through the repeat and continue the song.

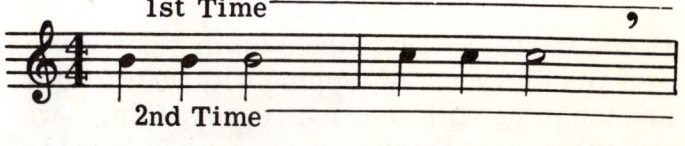

If the composer wishes you to replay only part of the melody, he will insert the repeat sign (turned the other way) ‖: at the point he wants you to return to the second time.

Here are some practice songs for the notes you have learned. Go over them a few times.

TWINKLE, TWINKLE, LITTLE STAR

BAA! BAA! BLACK SHEEP

RAIN, RAIN, GO AWAY

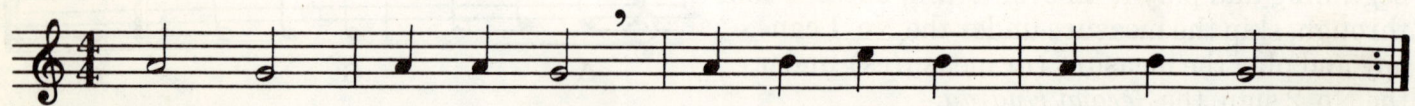

If you're still getting mixed up in your counting —if you find yourself tapping with your tongue and tonguing with your foot, or something—we can only repeat that as sure as aspirin is good for a headache, practice is good for counting. Go back over the exercises. Write some of them on paper and take them when you leave home. Hum the notes and beat out the time.

Session IV

Now we have the honor of introducing you to the *Eighth Note* (♪ ♫). What is it? It's half of a quarter note. It's a quarter note to which a tail has been added. Two of them together equal a quarter note in time. They are played in the same amount of time: *One Beat*.

This is done by splitting the note in half. Remember the little graph we used earlier to demonstrate one beat?

With the eighth note you make one note on the *downstroke* and one on the *upstroke*. That makes two *Half* beats.

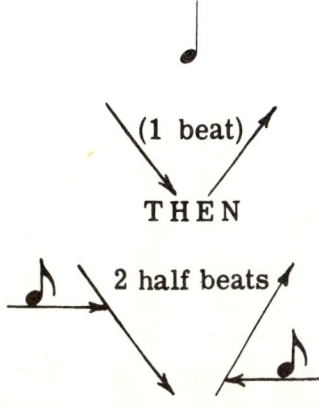

In counting the beats you've been using the words *One, Two, Three, Four*. To help fit those eighth notes into the pattern without losing the beat try saying, *One–And, Two–And, Three–And, Four–And*.

Get it? Don't carry the "one" all the way through the beat, but say "one" on the downstroke, then "and" on the upstroke, etc.

Once you have the beat set don't slow it to get the notes in. Keep the beat steady.

Ready to try it?

Count aloud, perhaps using your finger to make the downstroke and upstroke:

Down

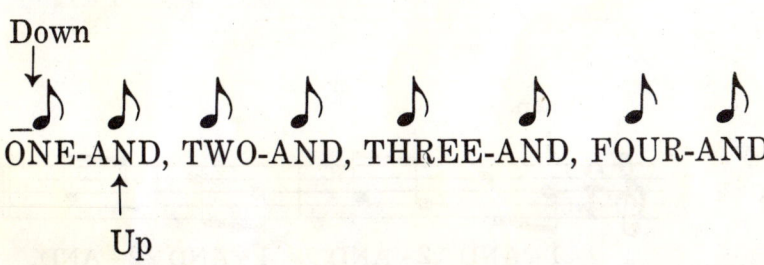

ONE-AND, TWO-AND, THREE-AND, FOUR-AND

Up

Do it over many times. Try it looking at the page, then looking away changing the beating to your foot. Substitute some silly words for *One-And*, etc.

After this has sunk in, bravely pick up your recorder.

Your eighth note "tu" will be half as long as the quarter note, with a break at the bottom of the beat as well as at the top.

Do this exercise until it sounds smooth.

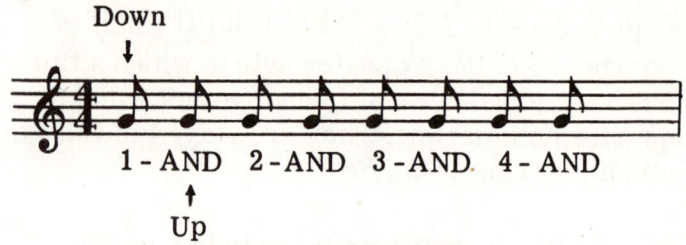

To save writing a great many "tails" and for better grouping, the composer often puts a *beam* across two (or more) eighth notes. It doesn't change anything. The notes are still eighth notes.

Summing up what you have done: The *Time Signature* states that in this measure you should tap 4 beats, with the quarter note getting one beat. You've done exactly that: played one measure of 4 beats with each quarter note getting one beat, even though you've divided the quarter notes into eighth notes. Eight half beats equal 4 full beats, right?

Now with your recorder, practice the same thing but change the pitch on some of the notes. Do it slowly, then faster.

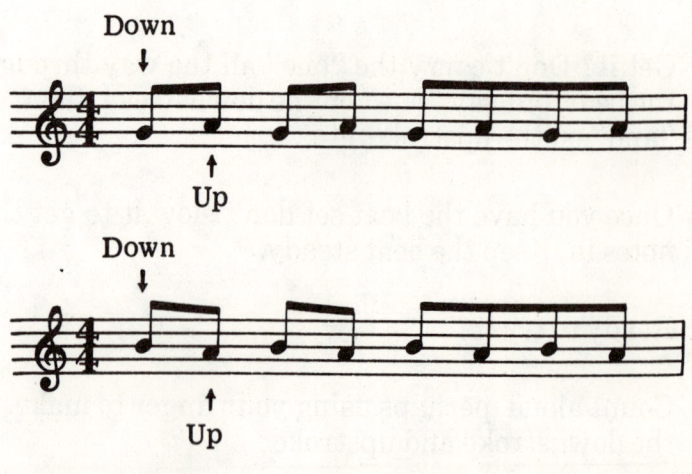

Now vary the pitch even more. Note the *Repeat Sign* (the writer's sneaky way of getting you to do it over). These measures are in $\frac{2}{4}$ time.

Meaning what? There are *two* beats to each measure and the quarter note (if there were any) would get the beat. So each eighth note still gets a *half* beat.

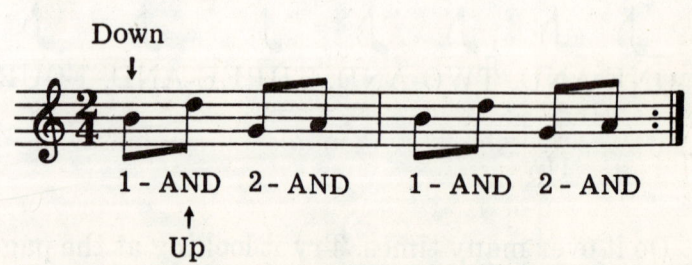

Go real slow here. You have more to think about. Count carefully.

Have you been watching fingering, good tone, relaxation? (Just checking.)

Once again, what does a $\frac{2}{4}$ time signature say? That there must be two beats to the measure and the quarter note must get one beat, right? It doesn't say that the entire measure must be made up of quarter notes, or eighths, or anything special. Only that they result in no more than two beats. So suppose we insert some different notes, making sure we don't go over two beats.

Looking at this new arrangement, what do we have? A half-beat (down), a half-beat (up), then a full beat (down and up). Total: two beats in each measure. Practice this a few times.

For your reward we'll tell you you're playing the first two measures of *Jingle Bells*.

Suppose we put a half note in the measure instead of the quarter note. Would this be right? Is it doing what the signature says? No. The two eighth notes equal one beat and the half note is two beats. That's a total of three beats. The signature calls for only *two* beats.

But since the half note *is* two beats we can put it into its own measure and it agrees with the signature. Play the two measures, making sure to hold the half note two full beats.

Now try them with variation in pitch.

Recognize them? They're the third and fourth measures of *Jingle Bells*. Let's put them together with the first measures and play them until they're smooth.

Ready to take the big plunge? Here's the chorus of *Jingle Bells*. All of it. Have fun!

Since you'll probably be playing a bit slower than usual you'll want to take more breaths than are shown. (Go ahead. We're big hearted.)

JINGLE BELLS

If you got through that without tearing your hair, you're on your way and should have no trouble with *Frère Jacques*. It's in $\frac{4}{4}$ time. Watch the eighth notes. You've got to reach high E while you're playing them. Go slowly. It will come.

FRÈRE JACQUES

There's one more bit of shorthand used in thousands of pieces of music called the *Dotted Note*. We'll creep up on the explanation through the back door.

Suppose we had one tone (say G) we wanted to last three beats, in one measure. Could we write it this way? No, because we said we had one tone to last three beats. The way it's written we have two tones.

We do it by using what is called a *tie*. It means "continue the same tone through the length of these notes."

Here we have a half note (two beats) and a quarter note (one beat). The tie makes them into one note for a total of *three beats*. Play it:

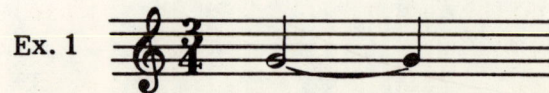

30

Try it another way. We'll add an extra note (and an extra beat) to the measure, so now we have $\frac{4}{4}$ time. Because of the tie the first note will last three beats and the second, one beat. Try it, and count carefully.

Ex. 2

There are hundreds of possible combinations for ties. Many times the tie connects a note in one measure to a note in the next. Play them as if they were one note.

(6 Beats)

Now we're through the back door and can discuss the *dotted* note. The tie is a form of shorthand, but there's even a shorter form of shorthand: when a note which is to be tied is followed by a note of *half its value*, a *dot* can be substituted for the *tie* and the *second note*. In Example 1 shown above we have a *half note* followed by a note of half its value, the *quarter note*. The quarter note and the tie are dropped and a *dot* is substituted:

♩. = ♩ ♩

Example 2 would be written:

♩. ♩

So, upon seeing a dotted note in written music, you'll know immediately the note is to be lengthened by half.

For instance, the dotted quarter note is equal to a quarter plus an eighth note, or, in terms of beats, one beat plus a half beat. The note will last through the *downstroke, upstroke, downstroke*.

Down   Down
↓   ↓

↑
Up
1-AND-2

If this dotted quarter is followed by an eighth note, the eighth note would be taken on the remaining *upstroke*. Count it aloud several times. (Remember: two separate notes, the dotted quarter and the eighth.)

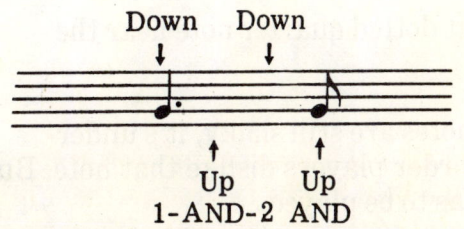

Down   Down
↓   ↓

↑   ↑
Up   Up
1-AND-2 AND

Since a dotted note is always composed of a note plus another note of exactly *half* its value, combinations such as these will not be found. Practice counting dotted combinations as much as possible. They're logical and will come with time.

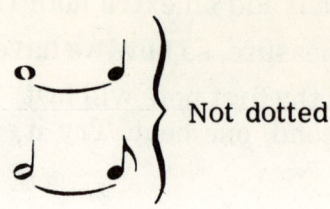

Now let's put it all together. In the following song both dotted notes and ties are used. There are plenty of *L–O–N–G* notes which may seem slow but they'll give you time to think. Breathing marks are included but need not be followed. Take extra breaths where needed, but make them quick.

OLD FOLKS AT HOME

Did you get that dotted quarter note near the end?

If those low C notes are still shaky, it's understandable. Recorder players dislike that note. But it's there and has to be played.

Work your way through this one. It's in $\frac{3}{4}$ (waltz) time. Remember, the accent is on the first beat.

ONE . . two . . three, . . *ONE* . . two . . three

In our next song you'll notice the first measure doesn't have a full three beats. This often happens. You still count out your "free" measure, but in this way: count two beats, then begin playing on the third beat (2 eighth notes equal one beat, right?). Observe the dotted and tied notes (both together in some cases). Count them carefully and play exactly what's written.

In the last measure there is an unfamiliar object, a *rest*. We'll take that up in the next rest period (that's some sort of a joke?).

IN THE GOOD OLD SUMMERTIME

Here's a song which will introduce a new feature. It's really a type of tie, called a *slur*. With a tie we connect notes on the same pitch. With a slur we connect notes of different pitch. Play the first note of the slur for its duration, then cleanly drop or raise the fingers for the second note, making one long note from one pitch to the other. A slur is a matter of style, so it's not necessary. But it sounds nice.

DRINK TO ME ONLY WITH THINE EYES

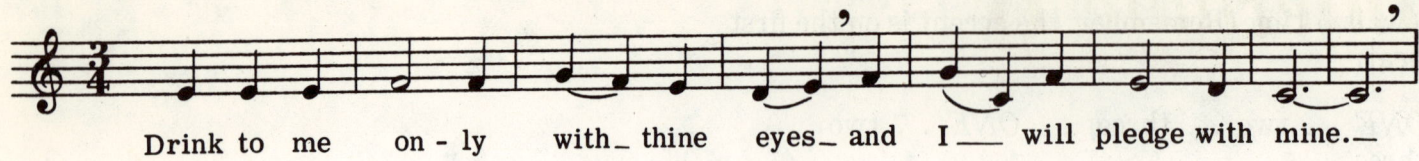
Drink to me on - ly with thine eyes and I will pledge with mine.

Or leave a kiss with - in the cup and I'll not ask for wine. The

thirst that from the soul doth rise, doth ask a drink di - vine

but might I of Jove's nec - tar sip I would not change for thine.

Interlude IV

A word about this counting business. You've probably found it difficult. You aren't alone. Musicians with years of experience sometimes find it troublesome.

This is one reason for having a conductor or leader. He keeps the rhythm.

After much practice you'll find you have developed, to some degree, a "sense" of the timing of the notes.

And also a timing of the *rests*. A rest, stated quite simply, means silence.

Each of the notes you've studied so far has a *rest* corresponding to the exact timing of that note.

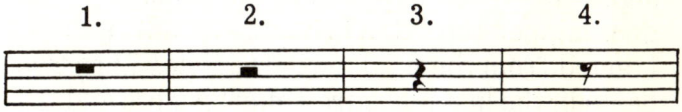

1) is the *whole* rest, counted with four beats of silence.

2) is the *half* rest, counted with two beats of silence.

3) is the *quarter* rest, counted with one beat of silence.

4) is the *eighth* rest, counted with $\frac{1}{2}$ of a beat of silence.

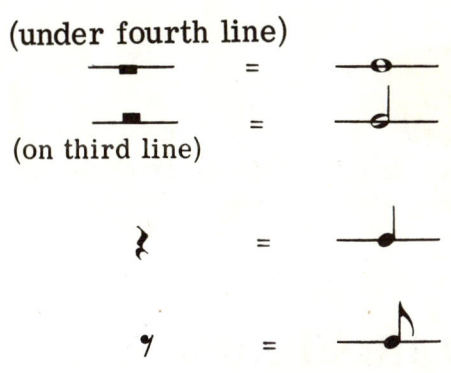

Each rest must be counted. Your tapping will continue even though you're not making a sound.

Here are some *rest* exercises. Tap them out "tum-tum" style first without the recorder, then play them. Remember to count all the rests, even those at the end.

35

You've got everything in this one: *rests, tied notes*, a *slur* and *dotted notes*.

ON TOP OF OLD SMOKY

Remember we said many songs start with less beats in the first measure than is indicated in the signature? This happens in *Old Smoky*. When it does happen the extra beats are usually subtracted from the final measure. *Smoky* has two beats in the last measure (quarter note and quarter rest).

Work your way through this old Irish melody by Chauncey Olcott.

MY WILD IRISH ROSE

36

We'll complete this interlude with a Christmas song, probably the nicest one ever written. All the dotted notes, ties, slurs and rests flow like water. You hardly need to count.

You'll find a new note here: High F. Look at the fingering chart. See anything different? The thumb hole? For high F, it's only half open. You squeeze your thumbnail into the hole, closing off half of it. Or rather, approximately half; you might have to leave a little more open, or a little less. Experiment until the tone is clean. And you'll have to reach high by constricting the throat and pushing with the diaphragm.

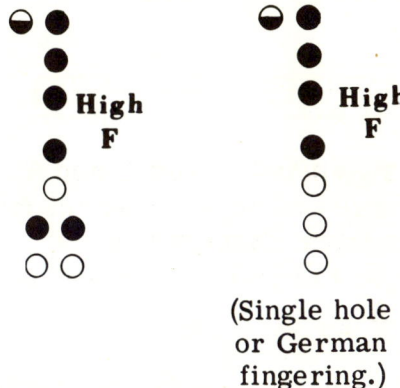

(Single hole or German fingering.)

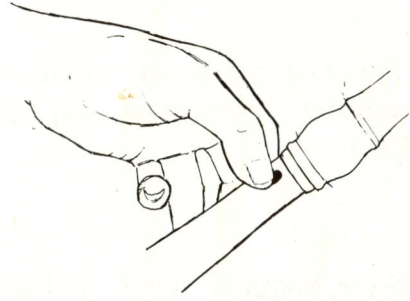

Notice that the fingering on the lower part of the instrument is different than for low F.

SILENT NIGHT

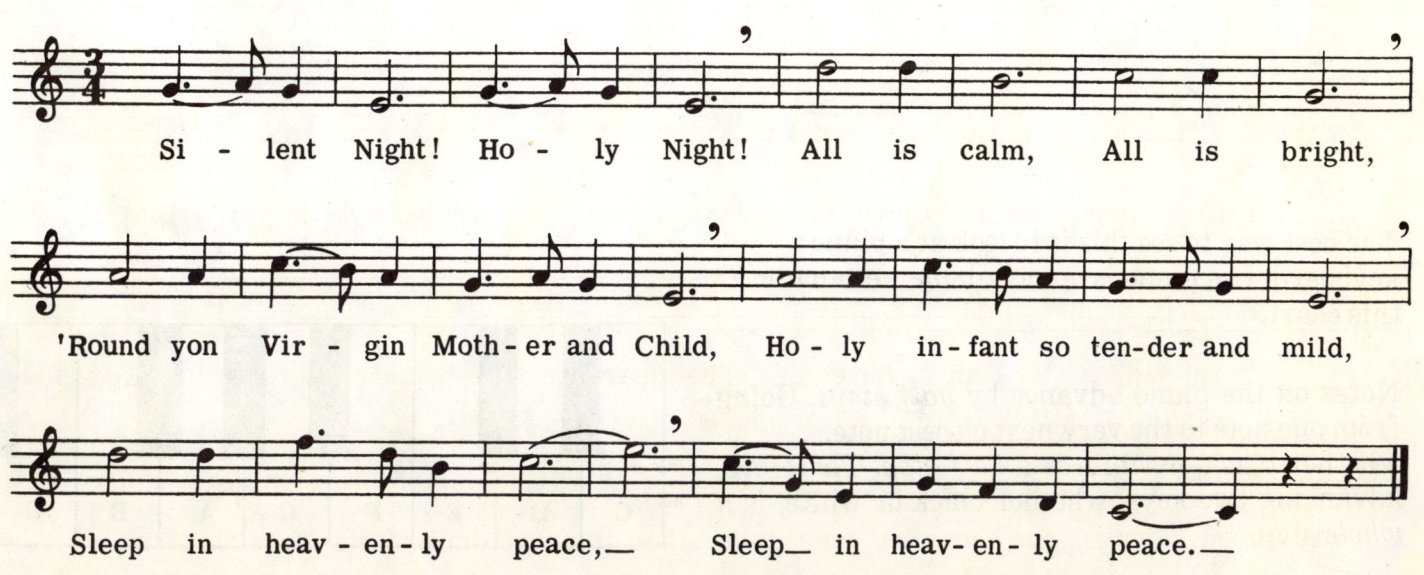

Si - lent Night! Ho - ly Night! All is calm, All is bright,

'Round yon Vir - gin Moth - er and Child, Ho - ly in - fant so ten - der and mild,

Sleep in heav - en - ly peace,— Sleep in heav - en - ly peace.—

Session V

We have two more high notes for you, G and A. That will be all. There are higher ones but most folk music won't use them. Eventually you'll want to learn them, so a fingering chart will be found in Appendix A.

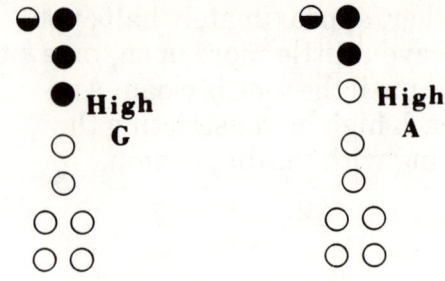

For G and A you'll probably have to squeeze your thumbnail a bit more into the thumb hole, narrow the throat "tunnel" and push with the diaphragm; not too much but just enough to make the note clear.

The adjustments for these notes vary with each person and each recorder. Experiment until you find what is right for you.

Pick up your recorder, begin on low C and play, step by step, up to high C.

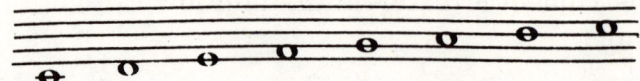

You've played eight notes (seven, actually, plus repeating C at the top).

As far as you know, the intervals between the steps in the C scale you just played are all equal, right? 7 steps, the same distance apart from each other? It would seem so, but it isn't true. There are some hidden *half* steps there.

The best way to see this is to look at a piano keyboard. If a piano is not available we can use this chart.

Notes on the piano advance by *half steps*. Going from one note to the very next closest note, whether black or white is a *half step*. Therefore, advancing two keys, whether black or white, is a *whole* step.

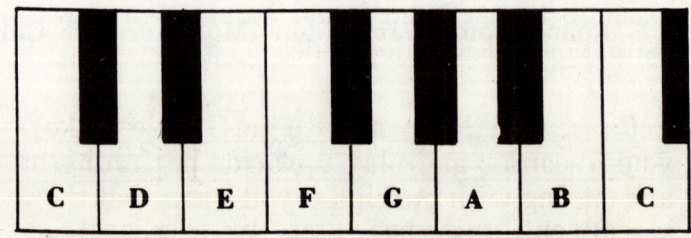

38

By striking the (white) C key on the left, and then, working toward the right (higher or up the scale), striking the black key, you have taken a *half* step. Strike the second white key now and you've taken another half step. If you had gone from the first white key to the second white key directly you would have advanced a *whole* step. Continuing upward, from D to E (white to white) you have another whole step (or two half steps: D to the black note, black note to E). But now, going from E to F, no black key is needed because E to F is a *half step*.

(Remember what was stated before: going from one note to the very next closest note, whether black or white, is a half step.)

Working your way up the keys you'll find that each step, from one white key to the next white key is a whole step until you come to the step from B to C. Here you have another *half* step.

Let's put it on the table where we can see:

All the steps are whole steps except between E and F and between B and C. Or, to use the numbers, all whole steps except between 3 and 4 and between 7 and 8.

On your recorder play once again from low C to high C.

Those half steps (E to F, B to C) don't sound like half steps, do they? But they are. We have heard this arrangement of notes so many times in our lives that we accept it.

When we have this arrangement—all whole steps except between the 3rd and 4th and between the 7th and 8th notes—we have a *Major scale*.

By playing from low C to high C on your recorder you have played the C *Major scale*. (Each scale takes its name from the letter around which the scale revolves, sort of like homeplate in baseball.)

Each note on the recorder has its own scale, but they don't all fit the C scale pattern. The point is that they must fit that pattern—all whole steps except between 3 and 4, and 7 and 8—or they cannot be called major scales.

Let's see what happens with the G scale. Take your recorder and play upwards beginning on G and ending with the high G you learned at the start of this lesson.

		Half step				Half step	
C	D	E	F	G	A	B	C
o	o	o	o	o	o	o	o
1	2	3	4	5	6	7	8

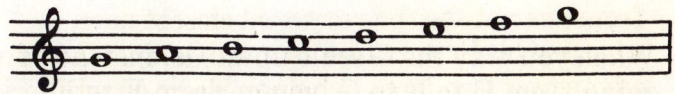

It sounds O.K. until you get up near the top, then it sounds wrong. Let's take the scale apart, note by note, and see what's wrong.

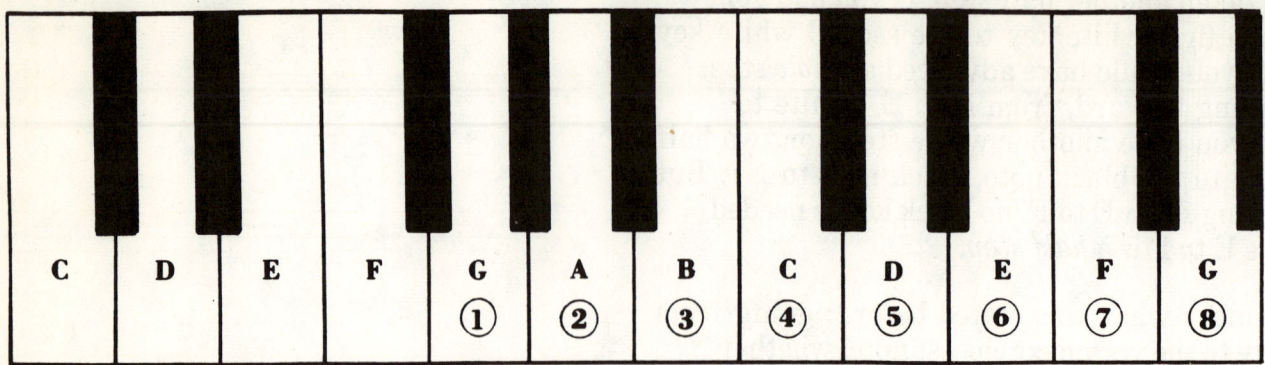

Check each note against the keyboard. Remember what we're trying to find out: do we have all whole steps except between 3 & 4 and 7 & 8?

1 to 2 (G to A) is a whole step. 2 to 3 (A to B) is O.K. 3 to 4 (B to C) should be a half step, so that's O.K. 4 to 5 (C to D) is fine. 5 to 6 (D to E) is all right. 6 to 7 (E to F) has no black key between, so it's a half step. But it's supposed to be a *whole step*. 7 to 8 (F to G) has a black key between, making it a whole step where it should be a half step according to the pattern.

```
              Half step         Half step
                ┌──┐              ┌──┐
                ↓  ↓              ↓  ↓
    G    A    B    C    D    E    F    G
    o    o    o    o    o    o    o    o
    1    2    3    4    5    6    7    8
```

There's the trouble. In fact, double trouble. 7 to 8 is not a half step as it should be. Also, 6 to 7 is a half step but should be a whole step to fit the major scale pattern.

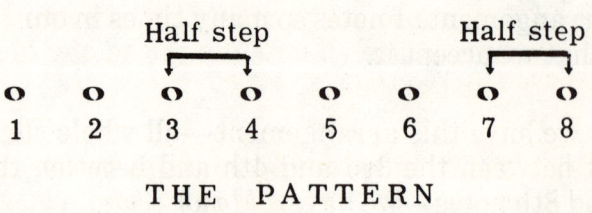

THE PATTERN

So our problem is this: we have to widen the space between 6 and 7 and narrow the space between 7 and 8. Refer back to the keyboard.

Suppose we go from 6 (E) to the black key on the right hand side of F. That's a whole step, right? So we've widened the gap between 6 and 7. It's now a whole step and fits the pattern. Going, now, from that same black key to 8 (G) is a half step. That's what we want from 7 to 8: a half step, so the problem is solved.

The name of that black key between F and G is F-sharp, or F♯ as it's written.

When you play the G scale upwards, instead of going from E to F to G, you go from E to F♯ to G.

40

Look at the old pattern:

And the new one:

The new one fits the requirements, all whole steps except between 3 and 4, and 7 and 8.

We now have the scale of G Major.

When you play a melody in which the key is G Major you must *raise* or *sharp* every F note whether high or low.

Here are the fingerings for those two notes on your recorder:

When a composer writes a song in the key of G Major he doesn't go all through the song and place a sharp symbol beside each F. He puts the symbol on the high F line, right after the Clef Sign. But even though it's on the high line, all F's must be raised also.

When you look at a new piece of music, glance up in the left corner to get your key. If you see one sharp you immediately know it's in the key of G, and all F's must be raised.

Now play the G scale several times as before, but this time use high F♯ instead of F. Also, you can play downward as far as low C, using the low F♯.

Try a song in G Major.

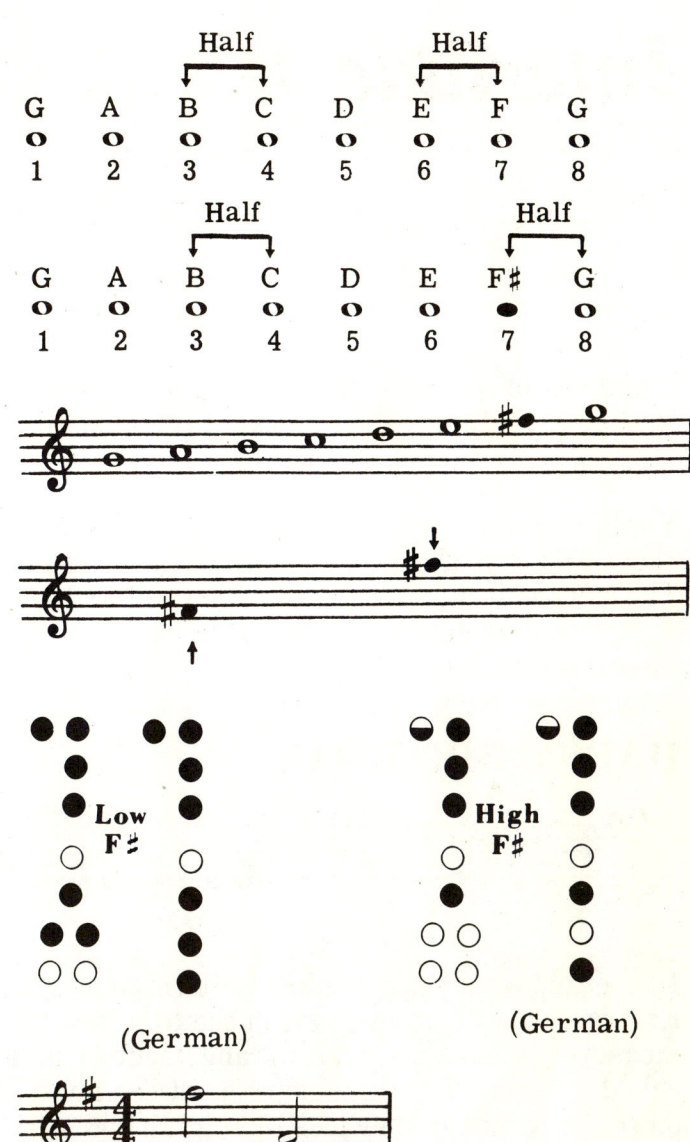

HOME ON THE RANGE

41

Interlude V

Hundreds of songs for the recorder are written in the key of G Major (sometimes abbreviated to GM or G). It's a popular key. Like to try a few?

You'll find a new symbol in the first one. It means "hold this note a little longer than is indicated." The rhythm is interrupted for a moment and then picked up again. The sign is called the *fermata* or *hold* (𝄐).

HAPPY BIRTHDAY

In the following song you have both high and low F#'s. Something new, too: in the first and fifth measures of the chorus an arrangement of notes called a *triplet*. The three notes must be played in one beat. Although they look like eighth notes they're not. Triplets will usually have a "3" over them. Time them so that all three notes fit one beat. (Move them a little faster to squeeze them in where only two eighth notes normally go.)

JUANITA

Soft o'er the foun-tain, Ling-'ring falls the south-ern moon; Far o'er the moun-tain, Breaks the day too soon. In thy dark eyes splen-dor, where the warm light loves to dwell, Wea-ry looks yet ten-der, speak their fond fare-well. Ni-ta, Jua-ni-ta, Ask thy soul if we should part, Ni-ta, Jua-ni-ta, Lean thou on my heart.

ADESTE FIDELES

Christmas songs make very good practice material.
 In the Time Signature of the next one a large C is used. It's often a substitute for $\frac{4}{4}$.

GOOD KING WENCESLAS

GOD REST YE MERRY, GENTLEMEN

Session VI

You've played the C Major scale (no sharps or flats) and the G Major (1 sharp). Are there more? Yes, indeed. Each note, including the half steps, has its own scale. Then there are other types of scales. But these are a bit far ahead of what we need right now.

It's necessary in some of the scales to raise more than just one note.

In the D Major scale (starting on D and going up eight notes) it's necessary to sharp two of the notes, F and C. Here's the fingering for high C♯.

For low C♯ we uncover one of the small holes inside the large hole at the lower end of the recorder.

Play the D Major (DM or D) scale both up and down.

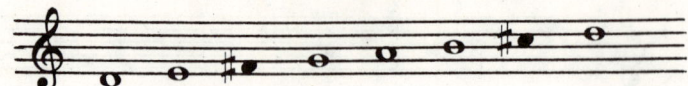

Try a song in D, remembering to sharp all F's and C's.

AMERICA

And this old Scottish favorite.

ANNIE LAURIE

When we go from one white key to the next highest note, whether it happens to be a black key or a white key, we are raising or sharping the note we just left. For example, we call the black note just above C, C♯.

When we go down the scale to the next closest note, we are lowering or flatting the note we just left. So, when we go to the black note just below D we have gone to D-flat (or D♭).

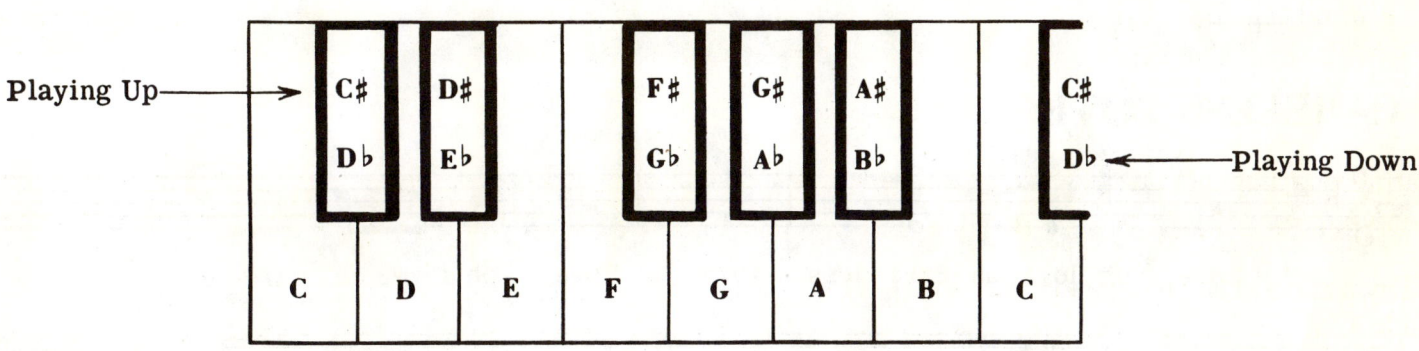

Look what happened: the same black note is the sharp of C and also the flat of D. It's C♯ and D♭. It has two names, the same as your grandfather calls your father "son" but you call him "dad". It depends on which direction you're coming from!

Can you find D♯? F♯? A♭?

How about E♯? That's right; it's the note we also call F.

45

In many of the scales it's necessary to lower or *flat* the notes rather than sharp them to fit the pattern. This is true of the F Major scale, where we flat the note B. Here's the scale, with the fingering for B♭ just below. Play the scale several times up and down.

Here's a song you've already played in another key. Play it in F Major. (In a later lesson you'll learn how to move a song from one key to another.)

HOME ON THE RANGE

A couple more songs just to help get your fingers around that B♭.

CARELESS LOVE

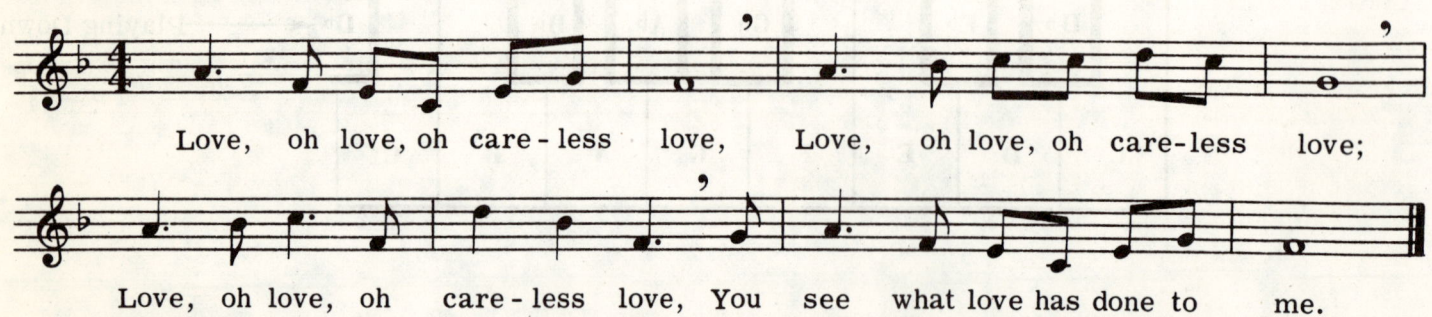

Love, oh love, oh care-less love, Love, oh love, oh care-less love;
Love, oh love, oh care-less love, You see what love has done to me.

BILLY BOY

Interlude VI

We'll call this interlude our "miscellaneous" period and catch up on some of the other signs found in written music.

To repeat what you have just studied: when the composer wants certain notes of the scales sharped or flatted he places a sign at the beginning of the staff. But he may wish to sharp or flat more notes than those indicated in the key signature. In this case he uses an *accidental*.

He puts an extra sharp or flat sign before the note he wants raised or lowered.

Try this on your recorder. It's in G, so the F is raised. The accidental shows that the B must be flatted.

The accidental applies only to the measure in which it appears. Similar notes in the measures following would be played "naturally."

Try this old favorite in the key of F. The B's would all be lowered if there were any. Since there aren't you have only to watch for the accidental.

NOW THE DAY IS OVER

This one is in the key of C but has two accidentals. Remember, they apply only to the measures in which they appear.

THERE IS A TAVERN IN THE TOWN

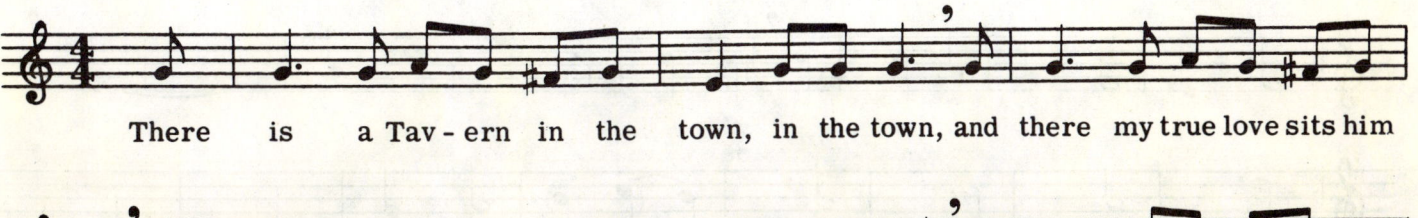

There is a Tav-ern in the town, in the town, and there my true love sits him

down, sits him down_ and_ drinks his wine as mer-ry as can be, and nev-er, nev-er thinks of me.

And one accidental in this:
FLOW GENTLY, SWEET AFTON

There's another sign called the *natural* (♮) which means "*Don't* play these notes sharp or flat even though this is asked for in the key signature. Play them naturally." The *natural* applies only to its own measure.

This one has two measures with naturals. (The second one affects both notes in the same measure.)

JEANIE WITH THE LIGHT BROWN HAIR

TOYLAND

There's one *natural* in this song.

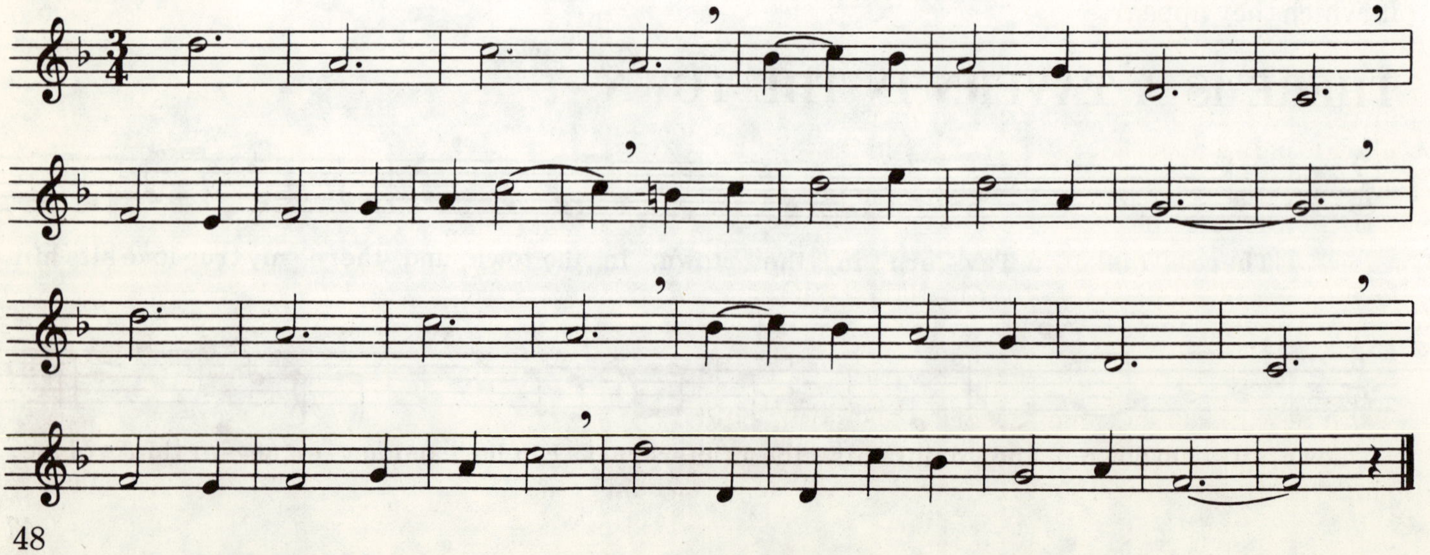

ID# Session VII

"How fast will I play it?" What's the Tempo?
It's a little like saying, "I'm outdoors now. How fast will I walk?"

It depends on what you're going to do, yes? If the eggs are frying and you've got to get back with the bacon, chances are you'll run.

You suit the tempo to the song.

A melody titled *Spring Dance* couldn't possibly be played at the solemn pace of *America*.

So to some extent your own feeling of what is right would be the best guide to setting tempo.

There are, of course, certain standards that are helpful.

Tempo can be set exactly to the wishes of the composer by the use of a metronome. If he wants his creation played at 90 beats per minute he'll indicate it near the beginning of the composition by stating that the quarter notes will be played at 90 beats per minute (♩ = 90). Then the player will set his metronome at that speed and follow the ticks of the instrument.

But most composers mark the tempo only generally and leave it to the player to be specific.

They'll write general words like *Slow* or *Lively* or use the Italian words, *Lento* or *Vivace*. The player, using these suggestions, would then choose the exact tempo.

In the early stages of playing the recorder you'll be playing familiar tunes and the tempo will be easily known.

With new melodies some attention should be paid to the tempo since this has a great deal to do with the "rightness" of the song.

A table of tempo and other musical terms will be found in Appendix B. You might also consider purchasing a Dictionary of Musical Terms for further reference.

We'll include a few songs here to acquaint you with tempo terms. Practice the melodies until you're familiar with them. Try them at different tempos until they sound right.

WHEN THE SAINTS GO MARCHING IN

LA CUCARACHA

GO TELL AUNT RHODY

Interlude VII

Music, they say, is an international language. So, in this section we'll let musicians of other lands speak. Some of the songs will be familiar, others will be unknown. Pay special attention to counting, accent and tempo.

The first song runs very smoothly and is great fun if you learn it by ear. It will take careful counting (all those eighth notes!) but you'll find it will come easily.

THE BLUEBELLS OF SCOTLAND

AU CLAIR DE LA LUNE

Session VIII

At some point in your long hours of practice you'll wonder what can be done to improve and polish the tone of your recorder. Time will do much to make it more satisfying but there are several things that can be done immediately.

If you want, let's say, a "sweeter" tone you can begin to think that way! Does that sound strange? It's what every musician does who interprets music. It's amazing how this helps the music; helps to round off those harsh edges and lets you slide in and out of those notes you'd like to sound "sweet as honey."

Work through this lyrical old number and try to play as softly and as smoothly as the moonlight and silver clouds over the sparkling sea!

SANTA LUCIA

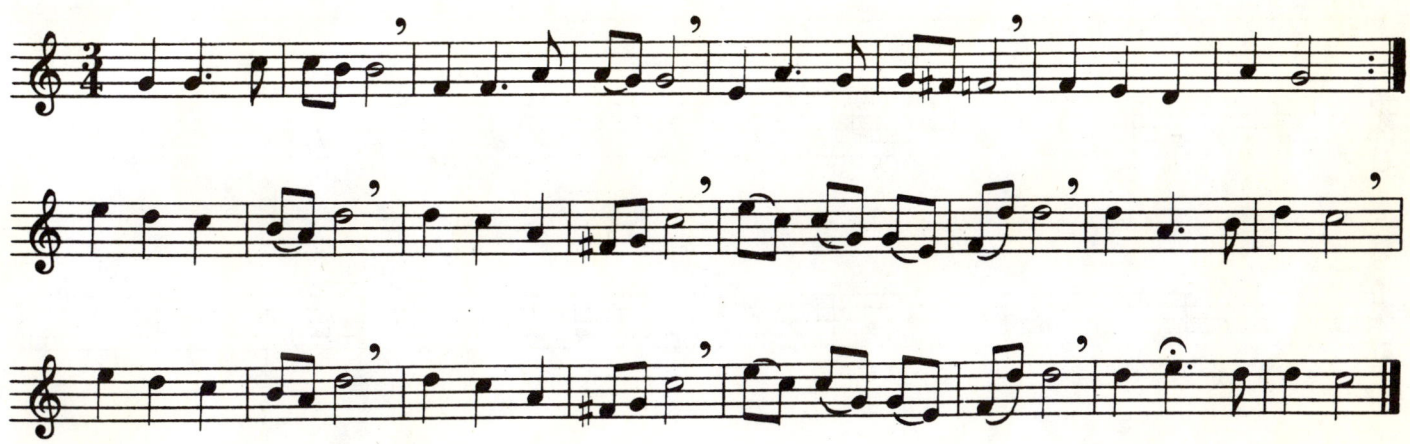

Of course every song is not sweet. If you're about to play *The Stars and Stripes Forever*, get your mind into that swinging, marching mood and make your recorder sing!

There's a special type of tonguing that might help to make your tones smoother. It's called *legato* tonguing.

Take your recorder and make a tone in medium tempo about a half note long. At the end of the tone bring your tongue back to its starting place so the tone is a long "tooooooooot."

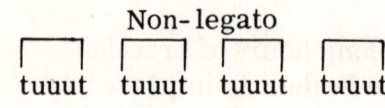

If you make a series of these tones, cutting off each one at the end, and then beginning another, you can see where there'd be a little "space" between each tone. This is called *non–legato* (or staccato, or detached) tonguing.

For legato (or close, or gliding) tonguing we don't want those spaces. We want each tone to flow smoothly into the next. So we eliminate the "weak *t*" at the end of each tone and begin the next one with the usual "tu."

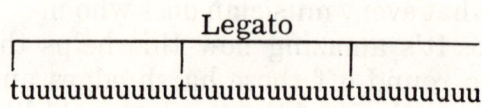

Try the legato on this waltz. Hold onto each tone and begin the next one without making an extra return trip of the tongue to its starting place. You will, of course, make the return trip at breathing places, rests and obvious endings.

Staccato tonguing is the opposite. You clip the tones purposely. Your tongue returns to its starting place at the end of each tone and a "tu" starts the next tone. Staccato notes should be very short. They are indicated by a dot above or below the note.

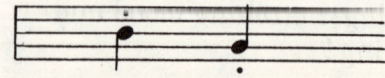

Try staccato on this melody. Clip only the notes marked staccato. The rest should be legato.

Still another style of staccato is shown in music by a short line over or under the note. This is also non-legato because there's a break between the "t's" but the break is shorter and therefore the note is a little longer than in the first staccato.

There's an embellishment done with the recorder which sounds excellent. It's called a *trill*. It's indicated by a "tr" over the note to be trilled. You do it by rapidly fluttering your finger up and down over a note.

The trill should be used sparingly and should not last beyond the length of the note trilled.

Go back to *The Bluebells of Scotland* and trill the notes marked "tr." Trills are not always marked and the player can find his own. See if you can find some nice ones here. Put in as many as you wish, but not too many.

THE HARP THAT ONCE THROUGH TARA'S HALLS

Interlude VIII

The smallest note you've used so far has been the eighth note, but of course even smaller ones exist. Frequently in folk recorder music you'll find the 16th note, occasionally the 32nd note, now and then the 64th.

There are two 16th notes to the 8th note and four to the quarter note. They're written like an eighth note with an additional *flag* or *beam*.

The 16th note has an equal *rest*.

A 32nd note and rest each have three flags.

And the 64th note and rest each have four flags.

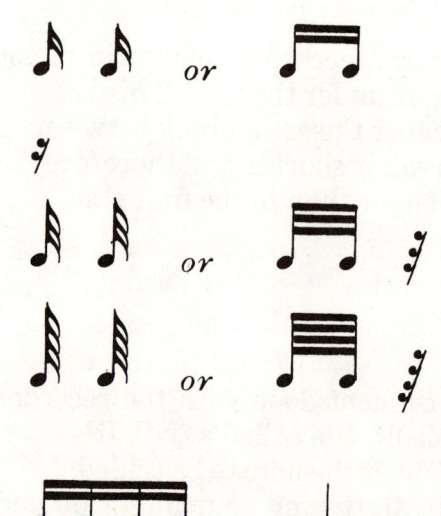

You'll want to spend time later in practicing these notes and rests but for the moment we'll include only one song using the 16th note.

Remember that if 16th notes are used, four of them must be gotten into the time of a quarter note, two into the time of an eighth. So they must be played faster.

A common arrangement of notes found in recorder music is two 8th notes divided this way:

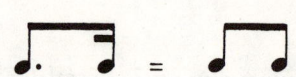

The dotted note is $\frac{1}{2}$ beat plus $\frac{1}{4}$ beat. The second note is $\frac{1}{4}$ beat. Together they get one beat, equal to two 8th notes in $\frac{4}{4}$ time.

ALOHA OE

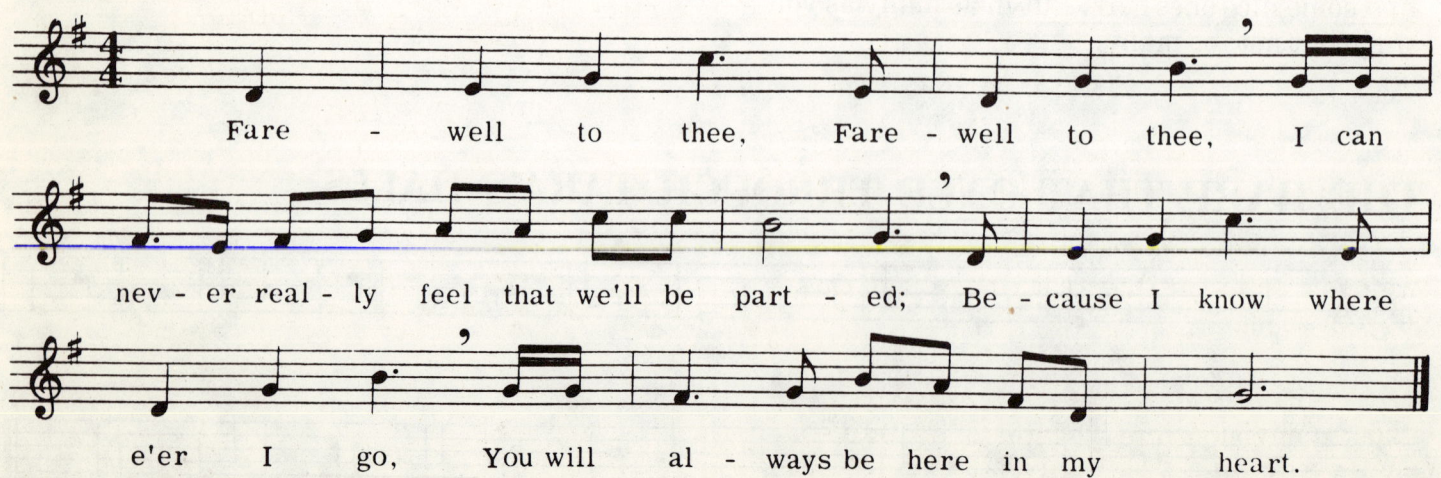

In addition to the $\frac{2}{4}$, $\frac{3}{4}$ and $\frac{4}{4}$ time signatures we've dealt with so far, there are others you'll find in music.

For instance, $\frac{2}{2}$ time means two beats to the measure with the *half* note getting one beat, not the quarter note; the quarter note would get $\frac{1}{2}$ of a beat. Instead of always being written $\frac{2}{2}$ it is sometimes indicated on the staff with a large C and a line through the middle. It's called *Cut Time* (𝄵)

By studying the measures shown here you can see that if you play a song with the half note as the basic beat at the same speed as one with the quarter note it will sound exactly the same!

Sound identical if played at same speed.

Cut Time gives a feeling of briskness and is intended to warn the player to play faster.

Here is a song in Cut Time. If you play it at the regular speed you'll see that the half notes sound like quarters, the quarters like eighths, etc. Start the song on the "upbeat."

LITTLE BROWN JUG

If a composer intends to use a lot of triplets he may subdivide $\frac{2}{4}$ time into $\frac{6}{8}$. There are still two *basic* beats but they each now have three notes in them.

Other subdivisions are $\frac{3}{4}$ into $\frac{9}{8}$, $\frac{4}{4}$ into $\frac{12}{8}$.

Session IX

We come now to the word *transposition.* Slightly terrifying, isn't it? It means, quite simply, moving a song from one key to another. Many musicians can do this at the same time they're playing an instrument, but we're concerned with shifting keys before playing the music. There are many reasons why it's good to know how to transpose. Possibly someone is singing with the recorder and can't sing in the written key. Or perhaps the written notes are too low for the recorder. Or maybe you just like the sound of a different key.

In this excerpt from the chorus of *The Battle Hymn Of The Republic,* written in G, there's one note (third one in) that can't be reached on the recorder because it's below low C.

So we move to the key of C where it can be played.

How? Very easy. First, pick a key which is higher than G (A? B? C? D? E? F?). We've chosen C.

Counting G as *one*, how many steps up is C? Four, right? So, everything must be moved up four steps. Your first note is D. Four steps up is G and that's where the song starts now. Second note is C. Four steps up is F (F, not F♯ since we're going into the key of C which has no sharps or flats). Each note is moved up in this way.

Easy? You can also count down. If the key is G and you want to go to F, everything goes down one step. Don't forget that if you move into a key which has sharps or flats you must sharp or flat the appropriate notes.

Transpose this song from D to F. The correct transposition will be found in Appendix C.

LOOK DOWN

Look down, look down,— that lone-some road,— be-fore you tra-vel on.
Look up, look up,— and greet your Maker,—'fore Ga-briel blows his horn.

Here are some songs you can play in the present
key. Then, for the practice, transpose them to
another key.

SWEET BETSY FROM PIKE

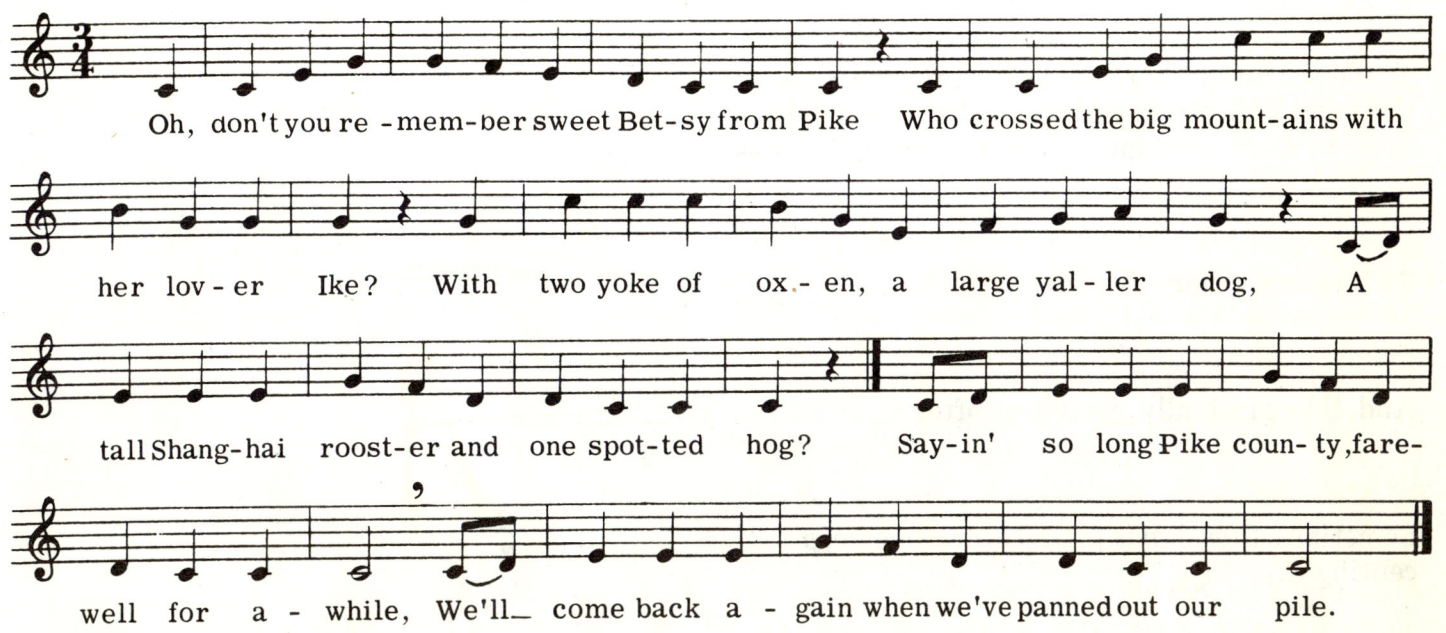

Oh, don't you re-mem-ber sweet Bet-sy from Pike Who crossed the big mount-ains with her lov-er Ike? With two yoke of ox-en, a large yal-ler dog, A tall Shang-hai roost-er and one spot-ted hog? Say-in' so long Pike coun-ty, fare-well for a-while, We'll come back a-gain when we've panned out our pile.

TAPS

Day is done, Gone the sun, From the lakes, from the hills, from the sky; All is well, safe-ly rest, God is nigh.

WINTER, FAREWELL

Interlude IX

You'll see many shorthand signs in your recorder playing. A Dictionary of Musical Terms will be helpful. Here are some of the more common ones.

This means gradually growing louder.

And this gradually growing softer.

Sometimes this sign is placed over one note, accenting it.

This means repeat the measure you have just played. (or, repeat it more than once.)

The letters *D.C.* mean go back and play from the beginning. If they appear as *D.C. al Fine*, the meaning is go back to the beginning but play only until you reach the word *Fine* (fee-nay) (the finish). Many songs end someplace other than the obvious end, as in this one. (Notice the repeat.)

THE ASH GROVE

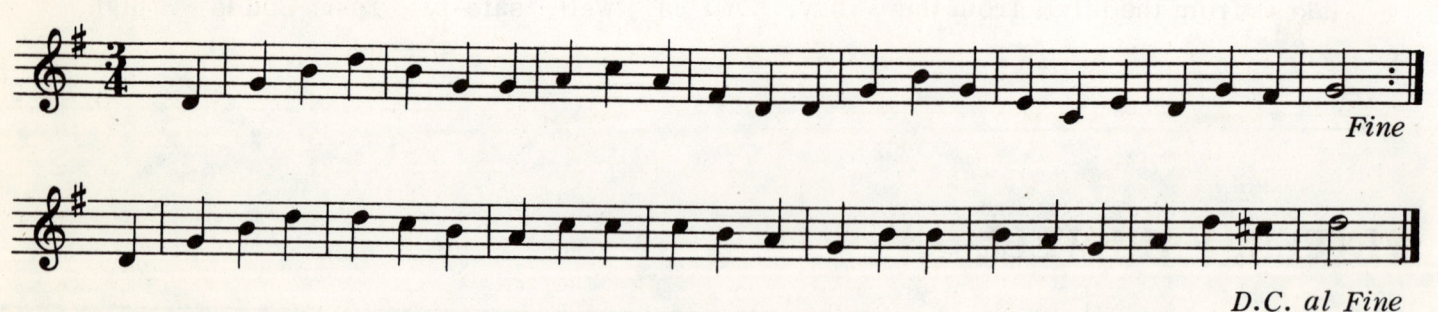

Fine

D.C. al Fine

If the composer had wanted you to go back only part way he would have written *D.S.* (from the sign) and would have put a sign at that point (𝄋).

Session X

A lot of fun can be had playing *Rounds* with a recorder. Two recorders can be used, or three, or more.

Round parts are numbered above the staff. Player A starts at I. When he reaches II, player B starts at I. When he reaches II, player C starts at I, etc. The song can be played through once, twice, or more. Or, at a signal, like a nod of the head, everyone can hold his note and stop the song at that point.

SCOTLAND'S BURNING

WHY SHOULDN'T MY GOOSE?

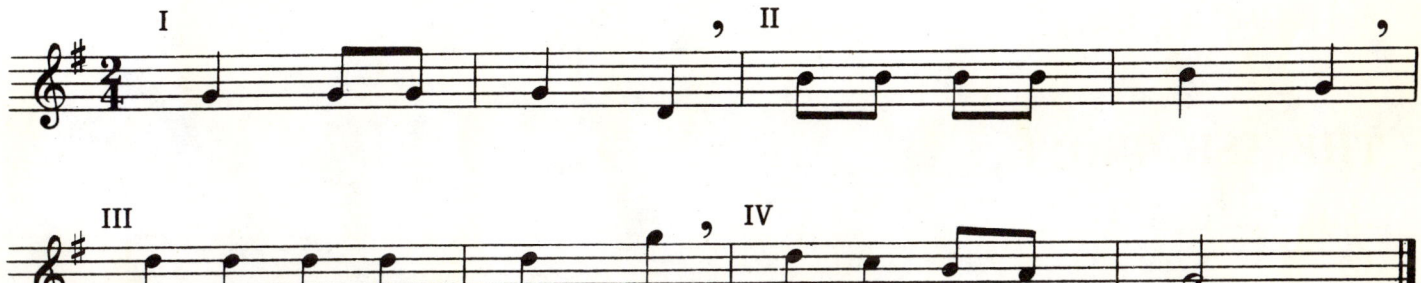

ROW, ROW, ROW YOUR BOAT

OH, HOW LOVELY IS THE EVENING

DONA NOBIS PACEM

Interlude X

Have you thought of trying to compose melodies of your own? It's fun and not very difficult because most songs are made up of only six or seven notes. Nearly everyone now and then has a strain of music running around in his head. Compose something simple, sound it out on your recorder, get it on paper and try to develop it. Use 4 measures or 8.

After getting all your notes arranged you might try setting words to the tune. Who knows, there might be a hidden talent within you!

Music is supposed to express feelings and emotions. Why not take some simple words like "I Love You" and juggle notes around until you have something that sounds well?

Rhythmic arrangements of words are always a good source of practice material, and one of the most rhythmic is Shakespeare. Here are some words from "All's Well That Ends Well." We'll give them a meaning different from the original (you can do that with Shakespeare!). They have a kind of holiday sound so let's make it Christmas and put some Christmas sounding music to them.

Make the coming hour
O'erflow with joy
And pleasure
Drown the brim.

Let's imagine you have a new addition to your family, perhaps a brother, son, nephew or something. Can you write a greeting to him? We need a name—Charles, Ed, Don, Richard, Glenn?

Glenn. O.K. Here's a greeting for him:

Welcome Glenn, hello;
Here you are, bonnie lad;
I'm your sis, see your mom;
That's your brother,
Here's your dad.

Glenn sounds Scottish, so we'll give the melody a bit of that Scot's lilt.

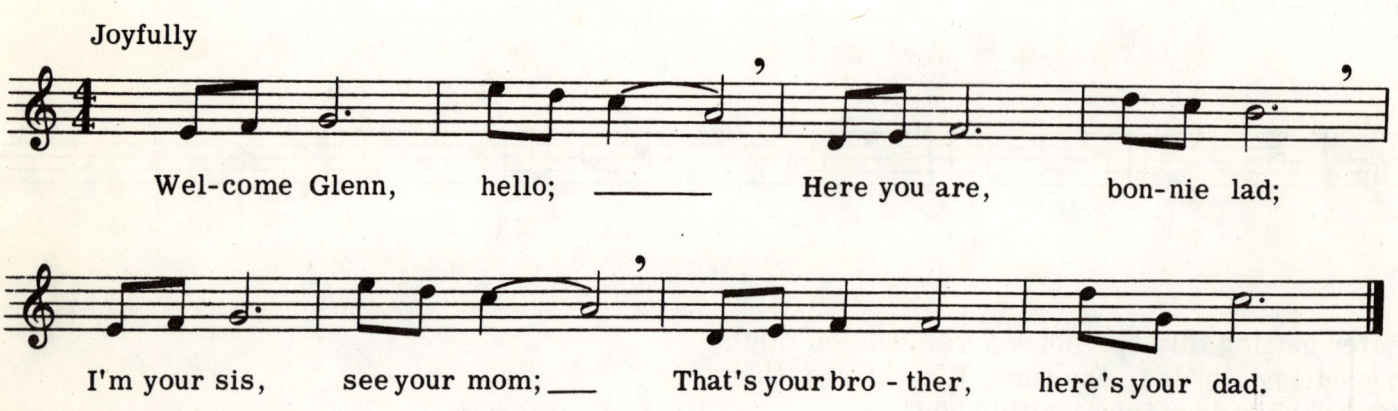

You can start with either words or music. Give it a try! Good writing!

Prestissimo	Very quickly
Presto	Very fast
Ritardando (rit.)	Slowing down
Sostenuto	Sustained
Spirito	Spirited
Staccato	Detached
Tempo di (Valse, Marcia, etc.)	In the time of
Vivace	Lively
Volente	In a flying style

Appendix C

THE KEY SIGNATURE

In this book you worked with the C, G, D and F Major scales. It was mentioned that there were many more scales. Each tone and half-tone has its own scale and it wouldn't be practical to go through them all step by step.

Each Major scale has a Minor scale related to it harmonically.

As you become acquainted with music you'll find songs played in keys other than those we covered and you'll want information about them.

A music teacher, musician or music reading friend would help, or you might consider purchasing a book on music reading.

This chart of the Major and Minor scales will furnish the basic information you'll need.

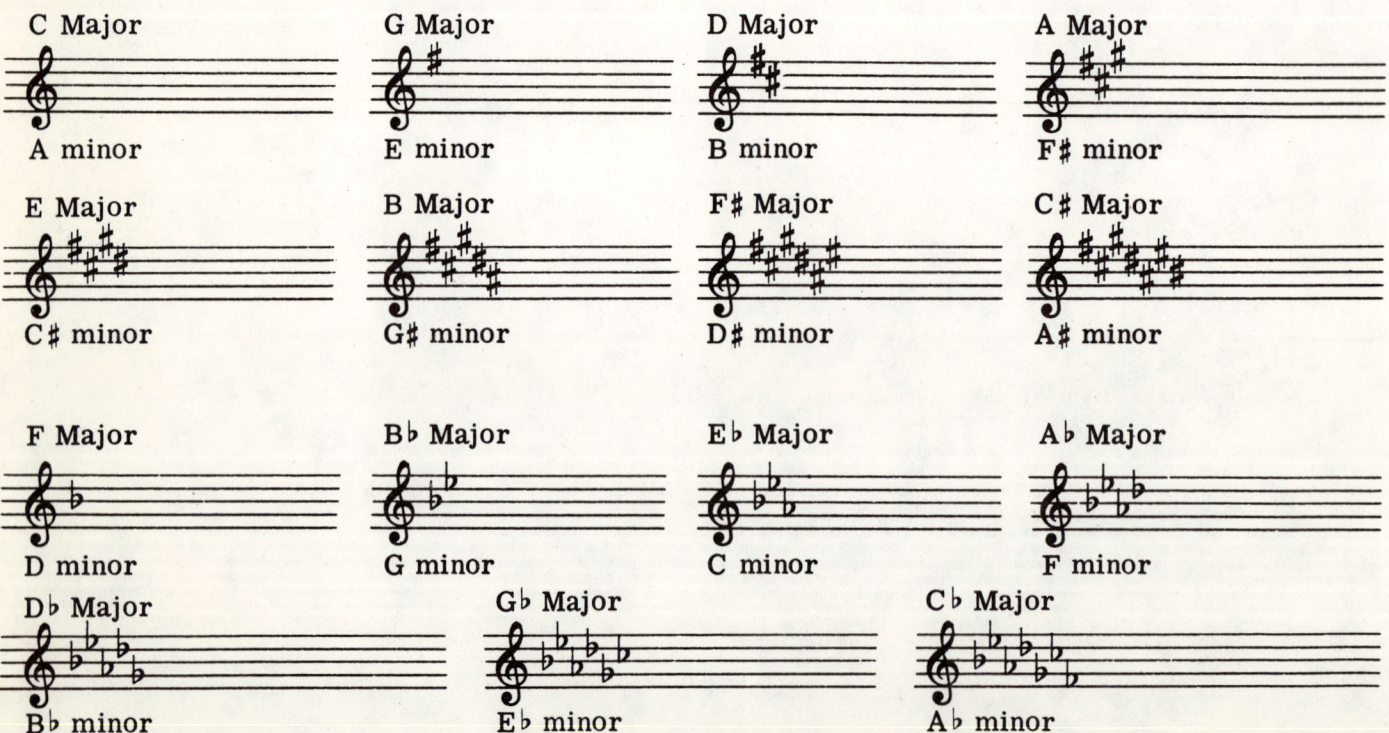

The correct transposition for *Look Down*, page 58

Appendix D

CARE OF THE RECORDER

Before playing your recorder, warm the mouthpiece in your hand. This will help hold moisture condensation in the windway to a minimum.

Most recorders are furnished with a swab. If yours is not, use a soft piece of cloth on a stick and wipe out the instrument after each playing. Be careful not to touch the delicate lip in the window. Damage to the lip will alter the tone.

When assembling the parts use a slow twisting motion to avoid forcing and damaging the joints.

If the joints become loose, wrap them with transparent tape. If they become tight, rub them with a light grease.

If moisture collects in the windway while playing, hold your thumb over the slot and blow the moisture out.

Wooden recorders should be treated with the care given any delicate piece of wood. They should not be exposed to extremes of heat or cold.

Read and follow the direction sheet enclosed with most recorders.

TUNING THE RECORDER

Instruments may vary slightly in pitch. For group playing, close tuning is desired. Have each person sound B. Listen carefully for the lowest sounding B. Then each recorder may be lowered in pitch by twisting it apart at the top (tuning) joint, thereby lengthening the instrument. Shorten and lengthen each recorder by small adjustments until all are tuned to the lowest B.

Bibliography

Bauman, Alvin, *Elementary Musicianship*, Prentice-Hall.

Baynton-Power, H., *How To Compose Music*, Pitman Publishing Co.

Bradford, Margaret and Parker, Elizabeth, *How To Play The Recorder*, G. Schirmer, Inc.

Best, Dick and Beth, *Song Fest*, Crown Publishers.

Duschenes, Mario, *Easy Duets For Soprano and Alto Recorders*, BMI Canada Ltd.

Hindemith, Paul, *Elementary Training For Musicians*, Associated Music Pub.

Hootenanny Song Book, Consolidated Music Publishers, Inc.

Hunt, Edgar, *The Recorder And Its Music*, W. W. Norton and Co.

It's Easy To Play Guitar, Consolidated Music Publishers, Inc.

Jones, Vincent and Bailey, Bertha, *Exploring Music*, C. C. Birchard & Co.

Krainis, Bernard, *The Recorder Song Book*, Galaxy Music Corporation.

Mirsky, Reba Paeff, *33 Favorite Songs From Gilbert and Sullivan Operas For Recorder or Flute Solo*, Hargail Music Press.

Newman, Harold, *Music Of The Hebrew People*, Hargail Music Press.

Newman, Harold and Newman, Grace West, *Music Shall Live!* Hargail Music Press.

Nitka, Arthur, *Anfor Recorder Method*, Anfor Music Publishing.

Nitka, Arthur, *Traditional Folksongs For Soprano Recorder*, Anfor Music Publishing.

Rigby, F. F., *Playing The Recorders*, Faber and Faber, Ltd.

Shanet, Howard, *Learn To Read Music*, Simon & Schuster.

Sing Out! Folk Music Magazine

The Trapp Family Singers, *Enjoy Your Recorder*, Magnamusic Distributors, Inc.

Welch, Christopher, *Lectures On The Recorder*, Oxford University Press.

Wollak, Henry, *Folk Songs From Here and There*, Alfred Music Co., Inc.